ISBNs: eBook   979-8-9921397-3-0
         Paperback   979-8-9921397-2-3
         Hardcover   979-8-9921397-0-9
         Audiobook   979-8-9921397-1-6
Library of Congress Control Number: 2024927232

First Edition
Book production and publishing by Brands Through Books
brandsthroughbooks.com

HiAnthony Media Publishing
HiAnthony.com

GRADE

· · · *A Memoir* · · ·

SCHOOL

ANTHONY MASSUCCI

To my mom, for always being there
for me and for all of us.
I love you.

To Robert and Donna... We are forever
warriors.

To Gary Vaynerchuk, for breathing life
into this project, telling me "write the
damn book!"

Contents

CHAPTER 1

Monster in the Front Seat

Pre-K

THERE WAS A MONSTER IN THE FRONT SEAT.

My mind was sure of it. I didn't dare move my eyes.

Sitting in the back seat, directly behind the monster, I looked at the rear of his head.

My peripheral vision calculated my escape. Our escape. There was none. We were trapped. I was trapped.

I couldn't move. I didn't dare move my head. He would see me if I moved.

Could I run? He would catch me. His strides were longer than mine. I was afraid.

I realized I hadn't felt this fear before, although this wasn't my first time with the monster.

With no escape, the only thing I could do was look him in the eyes. See if he knew I was afraid. Maybe I didn't have to escape if he didn't know I knew he was a monster.

My mind quickly calculated. *What should I do? Do I yell? Do I tell everyone? Say nothing and hope no one else notices? Pray he doesn't notice that I know?*

Suddenly, I had to go to the bathroom. I knew I couldn't leave. I couldn't ask to go. I had to do something. Time was running out in every way.

My mind decided. My eyes followed. I looked him in the eye.

Oh my god . . . his steel blue eyes were already staring at me.

I saw the monster inside him. I felt it with certainty. It was clear as he looked at me. His face was stern. Not a frown, not a smile.

Not a trace of evil anywhere. I inspected desperately. Deliberately.

I saw it now with my own eyes. I felt it for the first time seconds ago. Now I saw it.

Suddenly, my body relaxed slightly. I didn't have to go to the bathroom anymore.

I held the stare. *Don't hurt anyone. If you know I know, hurt me only.*

"Are you boys happy with your new names?" he asked as he broke our stare to look at the road.

His voice was slightly upbeat. My body relaxed somewhat in my seat. I was less stiff. My Spider Sense was tingling.

My mind raced. *How do I appease him?*

My older brother, Robert, was silent. Maybe he knew. Did he see the monster too?

He was in the back seat with me. He was on the right. I was on the left, behind our stepdad, Nick. The driver. The monster.

"I can spell it," I said. His eyes were now looking at mine again in the rearview mirror.

"S-q-u-i-c-c-i-a-r-i-n-i," I said with some confidence. I sat up slightly, holding his stare.

"Yes, that's correct," he said. He was surprised. I could hear it in his voice. I had fed the monster.

The car was silent again. The monster returned his gaze to the road, and I was left with my thoughts.

I realized I may be the only one who saw he was a monster. I wondered how long we had to be in this car, how much longer I had to be this close to him.

I could hear the hum of the engine, the sound of the tires on the pavement, but it was all distant, like a muted background to the building fear in my head.

In the passenger seat of the car was my younger sister, Donna. She was one and in the lap of our mom, seated next to the monster. My mom and he had Donna last year.

My brother, Robert, was six years old, two years older than me. Robert still hadn't said anything. I glanced at him from the corner of my eye, trying to gauge his reaction without moving too much. His face was pale, his eyes fixed on the window. *Is he seeing the same thing I am? Does he know we're in danger?* I wanted to ask or reach out to him, but I was too scared to move.

The monster spoke again, his voice breaking the long silence. "You boys are going to love your new school," he said. His tone was cheerful, almost fatherly, but I knew better. It was a mask he wore to deceive us. "It's got a big playground and lots of new friends to make."

I didn't respond. I couldn't. My throat felt tight, my mouth dry. I just kept staring at the back of his head, my mind racing. *What should I do? How can I protect my brother and myself?* The car seemed to be moving slower, each minute stretching into eternity. Suddenly, the monster turned on the radio. A cheerful tune filled the car.

The song "Here Comes the Sun" by the Beatles was the opposite of the tension that filled the space.

I felt my heart pounding lightly in my chest, my hands slightly shaky. I clenched them into fists, trying to steady myself. The song was a happy one, something about sunshine coming. Oddly, it made the situation even scarier.

I glanced at my brother again. He was still staring out the window, his face a mask of fear.

As I looked at Robert's face, I realized he saw Nick was a monster too. The thought gave me comfort. I could talk to Robert about it once we got out of this car. If we got out of this car. My brain was still feeling fear, knowing there was a monster in our car.

I wondered if he knew and if so, for how long? When did he see it for the first time? Was he afraid to tell me? *I don't care,* I thought. I just felt bad that my brother had to deal with the same awful feeling that I was feeling.

I wanted to tell Robert it was going to be okay, although I didn't believe it myself. The monster seemed oblivious to our fear, or maybe he thrived on it. Either way, he kept driving, humming along to the song on the radio.

"You're going to have so much fun," he said again, louder this time, as if trying to convince us. "Just wait until you see the playground. It's huge!"

I nodded slightly, hoping to appease him. My mind was still working overtime. There had to be a way out of this. Maybe if I could distract him, get him to stop the car.

But how? I needed a plan, something that would work.

As we drove, the scenery outside changed. Trees lined the road, their branches forming a canopy overhead. It was beautiful, in a way, but it also felt like we were moving deeper into a trap. The further we went, the less chance we had of finding help. I missed the South Florida palm trees. Now the trees were deeper greens and made shadows around us.

"Look at the trees," the monster said, pointing. "Aren't they beautiful?"

I nodded again, my eyes darting to the side mirror. Maybe I could signal to another driver, get someone to notice us. The road was empty, no other cars in sight. It was just us and the monster, isolated in this moving car that had us trapped.

My brother finally spoke, his voice barely above a whisper. "Where are we going?" he asked, his eyes wide with fear.

The monster glanced at him in the rearview mirror, a smile playing at the corners of his mouth. "I told you. To your new school. It's a bit of a drive, but we'll be there soon."

I could see my brother's hands gripping the edge of his seat. Was he as scared as I was? More? I needed to be brave for him.

Find a way to protect him. But how? The monster was bigger and stronger, and we were trapped in the car with no escape.

As the sun began to set, casting long shadows across the road, I knew I had to do something. Time was running out. I took a deep breath, steeling myself. I had to find a way to stop the monster, to somehow save us.

I looked at the monster again, trying to find any weakness. His eyes were focused on the road, his hands steady on the wheel. He seemed calm, in control. But everyone has a weakness.

I thought about the Hulk, my favorite superhero. What would he do if he were in this situation?

My mind searched for an idea. Maybe I could create a distraction. But that could be dangerous—for all of us. I needed something safer, something that would get him to stop the car without putting us in more danger.

Then it hit me. I decided to be brave for me and my brother and take a risk.

When the Hulk is not the Hulk, he is Bruce Banner, a smart scientist.

What would he do? I asked myself. I thought about an issue of the Hulk that I had just read where Bruce Banner had a very clever way of dealing with the villain. He had used his words. His brain and his words.

"I bet you were really good at school," I said, my voice faint.

The monster glanced at me in the mirror, a smug smile on his face.

"I was," he said. "Top of my class."

"Wow," I said, trying to sound impressed. "That must have been hard work."

"It was," he said, his voice full of pride. "But it was worth it."

I nodded, my mind still working. I needed to keep him

talking, keep him distracted. "What did you study in school?" I asked, hoping to keep the conversation going.

"Lots of things," he said, waving his hand dismissively. "Math, science, literature."

"That's amazing," I said, forcing a smile. "I hope I can be as smart as you one day."

He laughed. The sound sent chills down my spine. "Maybe you will," he said. "If you work hard."

I nodded again, trying to hide my fear. "Do you have any tips?" I asked. "For doing well in school?"

He looked at me again, his eyes cold. "Just work hard," he said. "And don't get distracted."

Distracted? Did he know I was trying to distract him? How did he know to say that?

I nodded, swallowing hard. "I won't," I said. "I'll work really hard."

He smiled again, turning his attention back to the road. "Good," he said. "That's what I like to hear."

I took a deep breath, my mind still racing.

I realized that there was no way to stop him. I was going to have to get along with this monster for the good of my brother and sister, and especially our mother. If we ever got out of this, it would be because she saw that he was a monster.

I felt the fear and thought that if I felt it and my brother felt it, eventually my mom would too. Or would she?

For now, I needed to find a way to save my brother and myself from the monster in the front seat.

CHAPTER 2

Peanut Butter Toast

Kindergarten

I WAS CONFUSED. SOMEHOW, THEY WERE BOTH SITTING AT THE kitchen table. Eating peanut butter toast.

I loved the smell of toast. I loved peanut butter.

It smelled good in the kitchen, but nothing could change the dread in my stomach.

I felt awful.

I couldn't believe it. I didn't know how this had happened.

Why would the monster be back at our kitchen table when we knew he was a monster? Did Mom let him in and sit with him at the kitchen table because he promised to no longer be a monster?

I wasn't the only one who knew. Now we all knew. It had been a year since I realized he was a monster. He rampaged against me, my brother, and our mom when he got drunk—and angry.

Mom kicked him out and told him to never come back, and he said he wouldn't.

But now he was at the kitchen table eating peanut butter toast.

How did he get back in?

The radio was on in the kitchen. It felt extra loud.

"This is Rick Shaw on W-A-X-Y, WAAAXY 106, with 'Surfer Girl,' by the Beach Boys," the radio announcer said. The jingle played, "WAXY106! Home of the Oldies."

I looked at them, both smiling. They were so happy.

"It's like a new beginning for us, Nick," Mom said to him.

"I'm telling you, Jackie, this time it's for good," Nick said.

"The hospital was just what I needed. I'm cured."

My mind raced. *He's cured? Of what?? What hospital?*

I tried to see inside him. Through his eyes. Into him. Was he truly cured?

"Just me and you and the kids, Jack," he said. "Us against the world."

Sometimes he called mom Jack.

He sounded convincing.

"Surfer Girl" by the Beach Boys hummed through the radio in the background.

I searched with my eyes. Time slowed. I felt my heart pounding hard. I hated looking into his eyes.

I looked at him for a second. Fast as lightning.

Don't let him look at me. Don't let him look. C'mon, God, don't let him look.

I held my breath.

I wanted him to be this new Nick. Life would be amazing.

My heart wanted to let that feeling in. But my mind wouldn't let it in. It just wouldn't.

I wanted to believe it . . . that the old, fun Nick was back.

Anything but monster Nick.

I looked away quickly. Then I scanned to see if I could look back at him. He was looking at my mom.

They were talking. He was talking.

I looked.

I stared at him again, thinking he would hurt me if I looked right into his eyes. So I looked at his hair. I watched them laugh and talk, eating toast with peanut butter on it. Smiling. Chatting like old friends.

My mind wanted to believe it. It was trying. I was trying. I wanted to believe. But it didn't feel like enough. Something was not right.

My stomach said no, overruling my mind. I chuckled inside, thinking about how my gut knew better. I wanted to let out a small giggle but didn't dare laugh out loud. I thought of the time Alfalfa from *The Little Rascals* ate ice cream and a hot dog. In that episode, they showed the inside of his stomach using an X-ray machine at the doctor's office to figure out why his stomach hurt so much. It showed a cartoon hot dog wrestling the ice cream and slamming it down on a boxing ring floor.

Picturing this cheered me up for a second. But I didn't dare smile or laugh. I looked down at my Trax sneakers. They were navy blue with curved white stripes. They looked clean, I noticed. Why did it make me happy to look at my sneakers?

I decided to go into my room to read a comic book while the coast was clear and they were happy. While he was happy. But my mind wouldn't stop thinking about Nick, hoping he wasn't lying.

My stomach knew. It overruled my head. He hadn't changed. I just knew it.

My heart dropped at that thought, although not as much as it used to. I was used to this feeling of hopelessness.

I want to feel happy, I thought. *I know, I'll read a Hulk comic book.*

As soon as I saw the cover of the Hulk comic, I smiled.

I read it again for the fourth time.

After, I looked at my small stack of Hulk comics that I had bought at 7-Eleven. I loved when the new issue came out. I wished they came out more than once a month.

I realized I'd read all of the Hulks in my stock. *I need more of my comics back*, I thought.

My mom and Nick were happy. He was distracted.

I put down my Hulk comic. *If I dare walk close enough to the kitchen table where they are sitting*, I thought, *I can get into the laundry room.* Just above the dryer, on a shelf, were the rest of my Hulk comics. Nick had taken them from me as a punishment for singing too much one day in my bedroom. He asked me to stop more than once. I was doing my homework and forgot to not sing. I got a beating, and he took the comics. That wasn't fair.

While they're happy, I thought, *I can get a couple of issues out of the stack of comics and hide them in my room. I'll read them when he's not around. I'll just take a couple. He won't notice.*

At least I hoped he wouldn't.

I got up from my bed and walked down the hallway. I made my way slowly toward the kitchen. I didn't want to make noise in any way or alert them somehow. I walked extra slowly as I crossed into the kitchen. I stopped. I was afraid.

I saw the kitchen table. They were still sitting. I realized they were talking extra loud and extra happily. He didn't notice me until I was close to the table. He looked at me quickly. As I glanced away, I saw there was no anger in his eyes. I looked down, as I did when I was around him.

Just don't make eye contact. Then he won't talk.

Walking faster than I usually did, but not so fast as to alert them, I went into the laundry room.

It worked! I was in.

I saw the comics in a white plastic garbage bag. I was shaking a little.

I tried to calm myself, but my mind was racing. If he heard the bag, I was doomed. If he walked in and saw me even look at the bag, would I get another beating.

I paused as I heard a chair move in the kitchen. Was one of them getting up?

I was frozen. I couldn't move. I was still shaking, but my body could not move.

If he walked in, I was caught. He would know what I was doing. He would know why I was there.

He's in a good mood now, I thought. I didn't hear any other movement in the kitchen.

I felt a burst of energy to go for it. I ignored everything I was feeling, grabbed the bag, and slowly pulled out the comics in there. They were all Hulks from that year and last. I quickly looked through them, grabbed three that I wanted to reread, and put the rest back in the bag and put it back fast, hoping it looked just like I had found it.

Luckily, it was my day to do laundry. My mom gave my brother, sister, and me chores six days a week. I pulled the towels out of the dryer. My job was to wash, fold, and put them away. I put the comics under a hand towel, fully covered.

I quickly folded the load of towels, one by one, straight out of the dryer. My mom had taught us how to fold clothes really well. If we didn't do it right, we had to put them all back in the dryer and start over. It made us really fast and good at it. When I was folding, I imagined I was in a contest to win first place.

I walked back into the kitchen, my heart still pounding from my daring retrieval. They were still laughing, still happy. I breathed a sigh of relief, clutching the towels with the hidden comics close to my chest. My sneakers made a soft squeak on the linoleum floor, but no one seemed to notice. I felt like a secret agent who had just pulled off a heist.

"I'm going to put these away," I mumbled, hoping my voice didn't betray the nervous excitement bubbling inside me.

Mom waved a hand. "That's fine, sweetie. Don't forget to put the whites on next."

I nodded and hurried down the hallway, back to the safety of my room. I gently placed the towels on my bed and retrieved the comics, sliding them under my pillow. My secret stash, safe for now. I couldn't wait to dive back into the world of the Hulk, where strength and justice reigned and where monsters were clearly defined and always defeated.

I sat on my bed, the smell of peanut butter toast still lingering in the air. The Hulk's angry green face stared up at me from the covers of the comics. I traced the lines of his furrowed brow with my finger, feeling a strong connection with the character. Maybe, just maybe, I could find a way to be strong too.

As I started to read, the words blurred together. I couldn't concentrate. My thoughts drifted back to the kitchen, to Nick's eyes, and to the laughter that seemed too loud, too forced. Could people really change? Could monsters truly be cured? I didn't know the answer, but I wanted to believe. I needed to believe.

The Hulk's adventures provided a short escape, a world where good always won over evil. Well, almost always. In the real world, things weren't so clear. I put the comic down and stared at the ceiling, uncertainty heavy inside me. The radio played in the kitchen, the cheerful sounds a bold contrast to the bubbly feeling in my stomach.

I rolled over and looked at my sneakers again. They really were clean. I smiled, just a little, thinking about how something so simple could bring happiness. Maybe it was the small victories that kept me going.

Tomorrow, I imagined I would wear these clean sneakers and maybe even sing a little while I did my homework. And if Nick didn't like it, well, I had my comics and my secret stash to lean on. The monster at the table might still be there, but so was I.

I lay back on my bed, clutching the Hulk comic to my chest, and closed my eyes. My mind drifted into a daydream, a place where the boundaries of reality blurred and I could imagine a world where the Hulk came to our kitchen. I pictured him standing tall, his green muscles bulging with power and his eyes filled with righteous fury.

In my fantasy, Nick sat at the table, still eating his peanut butter toast, when the Hulk burst through the door. The walls shook with his arrival, and Nick's eyes widened with fear. The Hulk's growl echoed through the house, a sound that made my heart race. Would the Hulk protect us from Nick?

The Hulk towered over Nick, leaning in close, his massive fists clenched at his sides. "You hurt Jackie and Anthony and Robert," he said, his voice a deep rumble that reverberated through the room. "And now . . . you don't get to hurt them anymore!"

Nick tried to speak, but his voice caught in his throat. He was frozen, just like I had been in the laundry room. This time, it was different. This time, the monster was the one who was scared.

"I want you to promise," the Hulk spoke, his voice softer now but still filled with an undeniable strength, "that you'll never hurt them again. You'll treat them kindly."

Nick nodded frantically, his fear visible. "I promise," he stammered. "I'll be good. I'll be kind. I swear."

The Hulk stood up straight, his expression softening. "Good," he said. "Because if you ever break that promise, I'll be back. And I won't be so nice next time."

With that, the Hulk turned and left the kitchen, his footsteps heavy. He walked with purpose. Nick was left sitting there, shaken but transformed.

In my daydream, from that moment on, he keeps his promise. He treated us with kindness and respect. The monster was gone, replaced by someone who truly cared.

I opened my eyes, and the fantasy faded. Maybe it was just a daydream, but it gave me strength. If the Hulk could scare Nick into being better, maybe there was a chance, even a small one, that things could change. Maybe the monster at the table could learn to be human again.

I picked up the comic book and started reading, feeling a little braver, a little stronger. My sneakers were still clean, the smell of peanut butter toast still lingered, and the radio played on. And somewhere deep inside, I held onto the hope that one day, things might truly get better.

When I closed my eyes again, though, I saw the monster.

CHAPTER 3

Miss Jones and Me

Kindergarten

I LOVED SEEING THE CAN OF "GENUINE CANNED FLORIDA SUNSHINE" on the shelves at the Gray Drug pharmacy near our house. It would always make me smile to think how someone took an empty can, put a clever sunny wrapper on it, and charged money for it.

I went to Broadview Elementary School on Bailey Road in North Lauderdale, Florida. It was a big school with lots of kids. I started kindergarten that year. My teacher was Miss Jones. She was really nice, and she always wore bright clothes that made her look like a rainbow. Miss Jones was young, probably younger than my mom, and she had a smile that made me feel warm inside.

At first, I didn't talk much at school. I was scared, not of Miss Jones, but of what might happen if I said the wrong thing. The monster at home made me nervous even at school. Things at home had gotten worse. Nick was mean, really mean. He yelled a lot and sometimes hit me and my brother. My mom tried to protect us, but she seemed scared too. I think Miss Jones knew something was wrong, even though I had never told her. She sometimes looked at me with a sweet, concerned look.

I remember staring at her calendar the first two months of school. September 1972 was etched in my head from staring at it so much. I just didn't want to make eye contact.

The calendar was my friend. It said October 1972 now. Looking at it helped me to avoid questions from Miss Jones, who had been asking me more questions.

She asked about my day, my night, and how I slept. At first, I didn't want to answer. I was afraid she'd tell my stepfather and things would get worse. But Miss Jones always asked so gently, like she really cared.

"Anthony, how did you sleep last night?" she asked one morning while I was drawing a picture.

I shrugged and mumbled, "Okay, I guess."

She knelt beside me, her eyes soft and kind. "Just okay? Did you have any dreams?"

I thought for a moment. "I dreamed about flying," I said quietly.

"That sounds wonderful," she said with a smile. "Where did you fly to?"

"Over the school," I said, feeling a little braver. "And over the park."

Miss Jones nodded. "That sounds like a fun dream. I like to dream about flying too."

Her questions made me feel like she was my friend, not just my teacher. I started to talk to her a little more each day. It was hard to share, but she made it easier somehow. She always listened, and she never got mad.

When I finished my work before other students in my class, Miss Jones let me sit in the back and read from her selection of books while I waited. Sometimes she would sit with me for a few minutes. One day, she asked me about my favorite things.

"Anthony, what do you like to do when you're not at school?" she asked while we sat on the reading rug.

I looked at the calendar—November 1972—and laughed. *That's a good sign*, I thought.

I thought about her question. "I like to draw," I said. "And I like to play with my little sister, Donna, and older brother, Robert."

"What do you and Robert play?" she asked, her eyes lighting up.

"We play with our Hot Wheels cars," I said. "We make a pretend city and drive the cars around."

"That sounds like so much fun," she said. "Maybe you can draw a picture of your city and show it to me."

I smiled and nodded. "Okay, I will."

"What do you play with your sister?"

"She has the best farmhouse and garage from Playskool," I said. "We play that all the time!"

"Tomorrow, draw me a picture of that," she said.

Miss Jones had this way of making me feel important. She always wanted to know more about me, and it made me feel good. I started to tell her more about my nights, even though I was still careful not to say too much.

Around Christmas, Miss Jones noticed that I was more comfortable around her. She said she could tell I was more at ease and happier in her class.

One afternoon, just after lunch, I came to her room a bit early and went to the back of her classroom. I stared at the calendar, December 1972, counting the days until Christmas and daydreaming.

"Anthony, what do you want to be when you grow up?" she asked later, while we were making holiday decorations.

I looked up from my glitter-covered paper. "I want to be an astronaut," I said.

"An astronaut?" she said, her eyes wide. "That's amazing! Why do you want to be an astronaut?"

"Because I want to fly to the moon," I said, feeling a little shy. "And see the stars up close."

Miss Jones smiled. "I think you would make a wonderful astronaut, Anthony. You're smart and brave."

"My Uncle Bobby was a fireman. He's smart and brave too," I said.

Her words made my heart feel big. No one had ever called me brave before. I started to tell her more about my dreams. She always listened with a smile.

After the holidays, I went back to school feeling different. Miss Jones had become my favorite person at school. I looked forward to seeing her every day.

One day, she asked about my family.

The question made me a little uncomfortable. I stared at the calendar and stayed quiet. It said January 1973.

"Anthony, do you have any pets?" she asked while we were working on a puzzle together.

I nodded my head yes. "We have a big dog named Snoopy. He's so loveable!"

"I love that," she said. "I have a cat named Whiskers. He's very playful."

"I like cats," I said. "Donna and I saw a cat in our yard. It was white and fluffy. Our house is right against the woods. We see all kinds of things."

"Maybe one day you'll have a cat of your own," she said gently.

I nodded, but I didn't say anything. I wanted to tell her more about home, but I was still scared. She seemed to understand, and she didn't push me. Instead, she talked about her cat and made me laugh with stories about Whiskers's silly antics.

By February, I didn't even look at the calendar. I wasn't so quiet anymore. I talked to Miss Jones a lot, and I even talked to some of the other kids. Miss Jones always made time for me, and I felt safe with her.

One day, she asked about my nights again.

"Anthony, how are you sleeping these days?" she asked while we were playing with blocks.

I hesitated, but then I told her. "Sometimes I don't sleep well," I said. "Because of the noise."

Miss Jones looked concerned. "What kind of noise?"

I looked down at the blocks. "My stepfather yells a lot," I said softly.

She put a hand on my shoulder. "I'm sorry, Anthony. That must be really hard."

I nodded, feeling tears in my eyes. I held them in. "Sometimes it's worse than that," I whispered.

Miss Jones took a deep breath. "Thank you for sharing with me, Anthony. I'm here for you, okay? When you want to talk, I'm always here."

I nodded again, feeling a little better. Miss Jones's kindness made me feel safe. I started to tell her more about life at home, and she listened with so much care.

As the months passed, Miss Jones felt like more than a teacher, she was someone I felt I could trust. I started to open up more, telling her about my dreams and my fears. I could tell she never judged me. She listened and cared.

One day, she gave me a book about space. "I thought you might like this, Anthony," she said with a smile.

I took the book, my eyes wide. "Thank you, Miss Jones! I love it!"

"You're welcome," she said. "I knew you would. You can read it and learn all about astronauts."

I nodded, feeling so happy. Miss Jones made me feel special.

Spring came, and everything felt new and bright. Miss Jones continued to ask me questions about my life and dreams. One sunny afternoon, while we were playing outside, she asked me about my favorite place to go.

"Anthony, if you could go anywhere in the world, where would you go?" she asked as we swung on the playground.

I thought for a moment. "I'd go to the beach," I said. "I love the ocean."

"Me too," she said. "The ocean is so big and full of wonders. Have you ever been to the beach?"

"We go a lot," I replied. "I like to build sandcastles with my brother and sister. We go to Pompano Beach Pier, and when it's crowded, we go to Fort Lauderdale Beach."

Miss Jones smiled. "Maybe you'll be an architect too, building big things like you build sandcastles."

I laughed. "Maybe. Or I could build spaceships."

"I can see that," she said. "You're very creative."

Her words made me feel like I could do anything. Each day, I shared more, and she listened. It was like a warm hug that wrapped around me, even when I wasn't at school.

April showers in South Florida meant more time indoors. Miss Jones and I spent a lot of time reading and talking. One rainy day, while we were working on an art project, she asked about my hopes for the future.

"Anthony, what do you hope to do when you're older?" she asked as we painted.

I dipped my brush into the blue paint. "I want to go to college," I said. "And maybe become an artist. No, actually, I want to become a scientist."

"A scientist? That's wonderful! What kind of scientist?" she asked, her eyes sparkling with interest.

"An astronomer," I said. "I want to study the stars and planets."

Miss Jones nodded. "I think that's a perfect dream for you, Anthony. You're so curious and smart."

Her encouragement made my heart warm. I felt like I could reach for the stars and actually touch them. Miss Jones believed in me, and her belief helped me believe in myself.

The next time I saw her, I told her I wanted to become a writer when I grew up. Maybe even a journalist, who writes about what he sees.

"Write for me today, when you're done with everything else," she said.

Here's what I wrote:

"The classroom at Broadview Elementary is colorful and warm. There are drawings and paintings on the walls, and Miss Jones's desk is always neat with a vase of fresh flowers. The room smells like crayons and glue, and there's a big rug in the middle where we sit for story time. Outside, the playground has swings and a big slide, and I love playing there with my friends.

"North Lauderdale is a busy place. There are lots of houses and stores, and the streets are lined with palm trees. It's always warm here, and the sun shines almost every day."

She hung it on the wall next to her chair. I was so proud!

As the school year came to an end, I felt a mix of happiness and sadness. I had grown so much that year thanks to Miss Jones. She'd helped me find my voice. I knew I'd miss her when the year was over.

One day, as we were packing up our things, she sat down next to me. "Anthony, you've done so well this year. I'm so proud of you."

"Thank you, Miss Jones," I said, my eyes misting up. "I'm going to miss you."

She smiled, her eyes kind. "I'm going to miss you too, Anthony. I know you're going to do great things."

I nodded, trying to be brave. "I hope so."

"You will," she said firmly. "Remember, you're strong and brave. Don't ever forget that."

As the last day of school approached, I felt a little sadder each day. On the final day, Miss Jones gave me a big hug. "Keep dreaming big, Anthony," she whispered.

"I will," I promised.

Leaving school that day was hard. I knew I'd miss Miss Jones more than I could say. She was my friend, my protector, and my guide. She helped me through the toughest times, and she showed me that it was okay to dream and hope for a better future. I knew I'd carry her kindness with me always.

As I walked home with Robert, the sun shining down on us, I felt a sense of hope. I may have been leaving kindergarten, but I was taking all the lessons Miss Jones taught me with me. I was stronger now, and I knew that no matter what happened, I could face it. With Miss Jones's words in my heart, I was ready for whatever came next.

CHAPTER 4

18 Rings

1st Grade

I WOKE UP FROM THE SOUND OF THE PHONE RINGING. IT WAS LOUD, cutting through the quiet night.

I looked over at Robert, who was already awake, his eyes wide open in the dark room. The glow from the streetlight outside filtered through our window, casting a mix of light and shadows on the walls.

The red glow-in-the-dark clock next to my bed read 11:45 p.m. I knew it was Mom calling. She needed a ride home from work. Nick, whom we called Dad, was outside, talking to the neighbor who lived in the house behind us. Both houses were up against the woods, as we called it, a giant wooded area that felt like it stretched on forever. The two men always talked late into the night, their voices a low murmur that carried through the still of the night.

Often, they would wake Robert or me with their laughter, which grew louder as the night wore on and they shared more conversation, beers, and cigarettes.

"Do you think we should answer it?" I whispered to Robert, my voice so quiet.

Robert shook his head, his face serious. "No. Daddy will get mad if he catches us out of bed."

"But what if he doesn't hear it?" I said. "Mom needs a ride."

The phone kept ringing, and we both lay there, frozen in our beds. There was fear with Nick around. Always a level of fear.

I started counting the rings in my head. Five, six, seven . . . I glanced at Robert, feeling more anxious with each ring.

"If it gets to 20 rings, we should answer it," Robert decided. "He can't get that mad if we're just helping Mommy.»

The phone was on its 18th ring when Robert and I jumped out of bed and sprinted down the hallway. The hallway was narrow, with paneling and a few family pictures hanging on the walls. The carpet felt flat and worn under my bare feet.

As we rounded the corner into the dining room, I heard the sliding glass door to the patio open. My heart skipped a beat, and I immediately bolted to retreat back into the bedroom. Robert was right behind me. He knew Nick was angry.

Nick answered the phone and spoke with our mom. "Yeah, Jackie, I'll come pick you up," he said, his voice lacking warmth. "Just want to make sure you are done for the night."

As soon as he hung up, we knew we were in trouble. We were stiff as boards in our beds, hoping beyond hope that he hadn't seen us get out of bed. Neither of us moved. You could barely hear us breathing. We heard his footsteps down the hall, shuffling with a familiar, heavy tread.

Nick worked hard. He hung wallpaper and painted for a living. When he came home, he wanted to relax and not be bothered by us. We knew to stay out of his way, especially after we had gone to bed.

His feet stopped moving.

Maybe he's so drunk he didn't see us, I desperately hoped.

He stood in the doorway, his shadow outlined by the dim light from the hallway.

His eyes seemed to pierce through the darkness, even though I couldn't see them clearly.

"What were you boys doing?" he barked, his voice low and menacing.

I peeked out from under my pillow, my heart pounding. I felt like I could choke on the tension.

We didn't answer, lying there, pretending to be asleep. But we could feel his gaze on us, cold and hard.

"Speak," he commanded. "I saw you out of bed!"

"The phone," Robert stammered, his voice shaky. "Mom called."

Nick paced in the doorway, the floor creaking under his weight. Then he stood still for a moment before pacing a few more steps. My stomach twisted.

"Did I tell you boys to get out of bed?" he yelled, his voice thick with anger.

We lay there, silent, staring at the ceiling, too scared to move or speak. The tension in the room was heavy.

"I asked you a question!" he said loudly, his voice echoing through the house.

Robert took a deep breath, trying to steady himself. "We were worried about Mom," he said quietly, his voice barely above a whisper. "Worried about Mom? I told you not to leave your beds!"

We got a beating.

After what felt like an eternity, Nick stopped. He was breathing heavily. He looked like a villain from the Hulk comics.

"You boys made the room smell," he snarled, looking so different, even more than usual, in my mind. "Take off your pajama bottoms and keep your noses in them until your mother and I get back from the Loft."

We did as we were told, too scared to do anything else and knowing nothing else would satisfy him other than what he ordered us to do.

I could hardly breathe. It was awful. My heart ached. I missed my mom so much at moments like this. I felt small, like an ant. I wanted to crawl into a hole.

When they got back from the restaurant, I heard the front door open and Mom's voice, soft and tired, asking how everything was. She walked into the room and didn't like what she saw. Her eyes went wide, her face tightened, and she turned to Nick, her voice rising in anger.

"Nick, this is too much!" she shouted, her voice firm and unyielding. "You can't treat them like this!"

"They need to learn discipline," Dad replied coldly, his tone dismissive, as if we were nothing but a nuisance.

"This isn't discipline. It's abuse!" Mom yelled back, her voice breaking. She was so upset. "I won't stand for it anymore. Not like this."

Nick stared at her, a flash of something dark crossing his face. But he said nothing. He just turned and stormed out of the house, the front door slamming behind him. The sound echoed through the night, leaving a tense silence in its wake.

Mom hurried over to us, her hands gentle as she helped us up. The warmth of her touch was a stark contrast to the coldness of the night. She went to our dresser, pulled out fresh clothes, and then went to the kitchen to grab a garbage bag and wet, soapy paper towels. She helped us clean up and get dressed, her hands trembling some.

"I'm so sorry," she whispered, her voice choked with pain. "This isn't right. I promise I'll make it better. I can't let this go on any longer. You boys deserve better. We all do."

She paused, looking at us with tears in her eyes. "I know this can't last. We can't live like this. I have to do something to get us out of here."

Her words hung in the air, a mix of determination and desperation. We could see the conflict in her eyes, the weight of the decision she was grappling with. We knew she meant it, but the reality of change felt distant and uncertain.

As she held us close, I clung to her, tears finally escaping my eyes. The weight of the night lifted slightly with her presence. As she cradled us, I felt a small comfort.

After she tucked us back into bed, she left the room quietly. I could hear her walking down the hall, her footsteps soft against the floor. A few moments later, I heard the front door open and close again. I knew she had gone outside, probably to calm herself down after everything that had happened.

From our window, I could hear Nick outside, talking to himself. At first, it was a low muttering, but then his voice rose, loud and angry. He was pacing in the yard, the gravel crunching under his boots.

"They think they can disrespect me?" I heard him yell, his voice carrying through the still night. "In my own house? I've had it up to here with this!"

The words echoed through the neighborhood, loud enough for anyone awake to hear. He continued ranting, his voice a mix of anger and frustration. "I'm the man of this house! They don't get to talk to me like that! Not my wife, not my kids!"

He was getting louder and louder, the anger and his voice rising. I imagined the neighbors could hear him too, the sound traveling through the quiet night. The whole situation made my stomach turn. It wasn't the first time he'd ranted outside like this. It never got any easier to hear. It was like he couldn't contain his anger and he needed the whole world to know how he felt.

I pulled the covers up over my head, trying to block out the sound of his voice. But it was no use. His words, full of bitterness and resentment, cut through the air. "They need to learn respect! I'm not gonna put up with this anymore!"

Nick's voice rose even more, as if he was addressing some invisible crowd. "You all hear me? I work my ass off every day, and this is the thanks I get? A bunch of disrespect under my own roof!"

I could hear Mom's voice too, softer and pleading. She was trying to calm him down, to bring him back inside, but he kept yelling, refusing to listen. The sound of their voices mingled, her soothing tone clashing with his harsh shouts.

"Nick, please, lower your voice," she said, her tone gentle but firm. "It's late, and the neighbors can hear you."

"Let them hear!" Nick shot back, not bothering to lower his voice. "They should know what I have to deal with. Ungrateful kids and a wife who undermines me!"

Her voice softened, trying to reason with him. "No one's undermining you. We're just trying to get through the day, Nick. The boys were only worried about me. They didn't mean any disrespect."

"They didn't mean it?" Nick sneered. "They didn't mean it, huh? Every time they step out of line, it's a slap in the face! It's like they don't even care what I say!"

"I care, Nick," Mom said, her voice got softer. "But this isn't the way. You can't keep scaring them like this. It's not good for anyone."

Nick laughed bitterly, a harsh sound in the night. "Not good for anyone? You think I enjoy this? You think I like being the bad guy?"

"I know you don't," she replied, her voice steadying. "But we need to find a better way. Yelling and hitting . . . it's not helping. It's tearing our family apart."

Nick was silent for a moment, his heavy breathing the only sound.

Then he spoke, quieter but still filled with anger. "I don't know how else to get through to them, Jackie."

"They don't listen. You don't listen."

Mom took a deep breath, and I could hear the strain in her voice.

"I'm listening now, Nick. But you have to meet me halfway. We can work on this together. We can make it better."

There was another long silence, the tension thick in the air.

I held my breath, waiting to hear what would happen next. Finally, Nick spoke, his voice tired and resigned.

"I'm going for a drive," he muttered. "I need to clear my head."

I wanted to see what was happening, so I slowly rose in my bed to look out. I could see them through the window facing the front yard. I knew they couldn't see me because of the angle.

Mom didn't stop him. She just stood there, watching as he walked away. The sound of the front car door opening and closing echoed through the night, followed by the roar of the engine. The quiet that followed felt heavy, like the calm after a big rainstorm.

I lay back down, my heart pounding, unable to sleep. The heaviness of the evening's events pressed down on me, a constant reminder of the chaos and uncertainty of our world. Like a drumbeat that kept beating.

In the stillness, I clung to the small comfort of Mom's promise.

I didn't know how she would make it better, but I had to believe she would find a way. She was the only one who ever truly cared and knew all that was going on in our dark world.

I knew I could only hope. So I hoped and stared until my eyes finally closed and I fell asleep.

CHAPTER 5

Get Solid Shorts

1st grade

IT WAS ONE OF THOSE DAYS. NICK WAS SNORING LOUDLY ON THE ugly green and black couch in the living room, right over the dark maroon carpet.

The couch was old, and the pattern looked like someone had spilled paint on it and tried to clean it up but only made it worse. It sat in the middle of the living room, a reminder of all the free, but ugly, furniture Nick's carpenter buddies had given us. Nick didn't care about how it looked; he just wanted a place to sit, drink his beer, and smoke his cigarettes.

I was playing with my toy cars in the hallway, trying to stay out of sight. Mom didn't want us making too much noise when Nick was around, especially when he was asleep or drunk.

Nick and Mom had been fighting a lot lately. Nick drank too much, smoked too much, and sat around all day. He did work as a painter and wallpaper hanger, but he wasn't excited about it. Sometimes he did shifts at the Sunoco gas station nearby pumping gas, but he mostly liked sitting on the couch, drinking, and smoking.

When Mom tried to talk to him about it, he'd get angry and yell. It scared me, Robert, and Donna. We tried to stay in our rooms as much as we could because if we were out of sight, Nick wouldn't bother us. Sometimes, if he saw us, he'd either ignore us or start yelling at us for no reason.

"Mom, why's Nick always so mad?" I asked, looking up at her with big eyes. She sighed and kneeled down to my level, brushing a strand of hair out of my face.

"He's just . . . unhappy, I guess," she said softly. "But you don't need to worry about that, okay? Just stay quiet. Keep playing."

A few months ago, Nick went to rehab. Mom was hopeful. She made us peanut butter and jelly sandwiches the day he came back and said, "We're going to be a real family. Nick's going to try hard, and we're going to make it work." For a while, it seemed like things might get better. Nick tried to help around the house and didn't drink as much.

It didn't last. He started drinking again, sitting on the couch all day on the weekends and most of the night after long days at work. The fights started up again. It felt like a balloon slowly losing air; everything slowly sagged back to the way it was.

I remembered the day we went to pick up Nick from the rehab center. It felt like a hospital, but with more people around.

I had been so nervous sitting in the car, dreading the moment we'd walk into that place. Once we went in, Mom walked fast, her heels clicking sharply on the tile floor and her keys jingling as she made her way quickly through the facility. Her voice was quick and determined, like she was trying to get Nick and get out of there as fast as possible.

The day we went, the Washington Redskins were playing against the St. Louis Cardinals, and I was so excited to sit in the waiting room, which was quiet with no one in there but me, and watch the game and escape from the weirdness of the place while my mom went to get Nick.

The place felt eerie, like everyone there was either brain-dead or drugged. It was so odd seeing people shuffling around or sitting with blank eyes. When Nick came out to meet us, I was shocked. He looked like a new and improved version of himself. There was a spark in his eyes and a confidence in his step that I hadn't seen in a long time. Maybe I had never seen him like this.

It was like he'd come back to life, and for a moment, I let myself believe that maybe things could really change.

I thought of that day as Nick was sleeping, or unconscious, on the couch. It was a Sunday afternoon, and the night before, he had fallen asleep there, spilled beer on the floor, and burned a hole in the part of the couch where we would sit. The smell of burnt fabric still lingered in the air.

I heard whispers in the kitchen. I slowly moved closer and saw Mom talking quietly with Robert and Donna. "Grab one outfit for school tomorrow and one to wear," she instructed, her voice trembling. I could see the worry in her eyes. It made my stomach feel tight.

"Are we going somewhere, Mom?" Donna asked, clutching her stuffed bunny.

"Yes, sweetie," Mom said, glancing nervously toward the living room where Nick was sleeping. "We're going to stay with a friend for a bit. We have to be quick and quiet, okay?"

I peeked into the living room. Nick was sprawled out on the couch, snoring loudly, with a Budweiser beer bottle in one hand and a cigarette in the other. I hated the smell of the cigarettes; they made the whole house stink.

Mom caught my eye and motioned for me to come over. She knew I heard what she had told my brother and sister.

"Anthony, get your favorite clothes, okay? And be quiet," she instructed.

I nodded, my heart suddenly pounding. I ran to my room and grabbed my favorite striped shirt and some striped shorts. I loved stripes, but as I was about to pack them, Mom stopped me.

"No stripes with stripes," she said, forcing a small smile, despite the worry on her face. "Get solid shorts."

"Okay, Mom," I whispered back, putting back the striped shorts and grabbing a pair of plain dark blue ones instead.

Robert and Donna were already dressed and ready. Robert, being the oldest at eight, was trying to look brave. He grabbed my hand and Donna's. "Let's go," he whispered. Mom was at the door, watching Nick carefully. He stirred a little, and her eyes widened.

"Go to the car, quietly," she said, her voice barely audible. Robert led us, holding our hands tight.

We moved like little ducklings, careful not to make any noise. Mom opened the door slowly, trying not to make a sound. We slipped out into the warm South Florida evening. The air felt thick and heavy, like a storm was coming. I could smell the coming rain. We climbed into the back seat of the car. I could feel my heart racing. My hands were cold and sweaty. I kept looking back at the house, afraid Nick would wake up.

As Mom started the car, the engine's roar seemed loud in the quiet neighborhood.

I turned around and saw Nick stumbling out of the house. He looked angry and confused.

"Jackie, get back here!" he shouted, his voice booming. He was yelling, waving his arms around, but Mom didn't stop. She backed out of the driveway, and almost without stopping, put the car in drive, hit the gas and drove off, leaving him standing in the driveway, shouting at us.

I could see from the rear window of the car that he stood tall for a moment. He looked looming and angry, just like the Abomination, a villain from the Hulk comics.

In the car, it was silent. I felt the tension, like we were all holding our breath. Mom was driving fast, her knuckles white as she gripped the steering wheel. After a few minutes, she spoke, her voice steady but with a hint of something I couldn't quite understand.

"We're going to Jefferson's to get some clothes, okay? Just enough for a few days."

"Are we coming back, Mom?" Robert asked, his voice small.

Mom sighed, glancing at us in the rearview mirror. "I don't know, Robert. Let's just... let's just get through tonight, okay?"

We pulled into the parking lot, which felt familiar. We'd been here many times to shop. Mostly for clothes. Seeing the big sign on the front of the store above the doors, "Jefferson Super Department Store" in funny-looking cursive letters, was like seeing a good friend from school. It felt familiar. It felt comfortable. *It's safe inside,* I thought.

Inside Jefferson, the bright lights and cool air felt like a different world. It was a place we came to sometimes, and it was comforting to be there, away from the chaos at home. Mom gave us a shopping cart for us to wheel around and told us to pick out clothes. I picked up a striped shirt and some solid navy-blue shorts, remembering what Mom said about not wearing stripes with stripes.

"Is this okay, Mom?" I asked, holding up the shirt.

"Yes, Anthony, that's good," she said, her voice softer now. She seemed relieved to be away from Nick, too. I felt a little better knowing we were safe for now. I spotted a pair of blue and white sneakers that looked cool and showed them to Mom. The soles of my Trax sneakers flapped and were starting to peel off around the edge.

"Can I get these?" I asked, hoping she would say yes.

"Sure, honey," she said, nodding. "Let's try to keep it simple, okay? We don't want to spend too much."

I nodded and put them in the cart. I wanted to help, so I decided to only get one pair of shorts and two shirts instead of the three she said. I figured I could wear the same thing a few times and no one would really notice. Robert and Donna were doing the same, picking out just enough clothes to get by. I could tell we were all trying to be careful not to ask for too much because we knew Mom was already worried.

"Mom, can I get this dress?" Donna asked, holding up a pretty yellow dress with little flowers on it.

Mom smiled and nodded. "Yes, Donna, that's a nice dress. Just remember, we need to be quick."

As we walked to the checkout, I felt a strange mix of feelings. I was scared and sad about leaving home, but I was also relieved. It felt good to be away from Nick, even if just for a while. He was like a dark cloud over our house, always angry and unpredictable. But now, we were out from under that cloud, at least for a little bit.

After we paid for the clothes, Mom led us back to the car. We all piled in, and she started driving again. "We're going to my friend's house," she said. "Diane and Stacey will be there, and you'll get to play with them."

Hearing that made me smile a little. Diane and Stacey were fun, and their house was always a good place to visit.

As we drove, I looked out the window at the passing lights and thought about how strange everything felt. It was scary not knowing what would happen next, but at the same time, it felt like a big weight had been lifted off my chest. For the first time in a long while, I felt like I could breathe a full breath. Even though everything was uncertain, I was glad to be away from Nick, the monster in our house.

We pulled into the driveway of Mom's friend's house, and I felt a little bit of the tension ease away. Mom turned off the car and looked at us. "Okay, kids. We're going to stay here for a while. Be on your best behavior, okay?"

"Yes, Mom," we all chimed in.

As we walked up to the house, Diane and Stacey came running out to greet us. "Hi, Anthony! Hi, Robert! Hi, Donna!" they shouted, hugging us. Their smiles were big and bright, and it made me feel a little more at ease.

"Come on, let's go play," Diane said, grabbing my hand.

I looked back at Mom, who was talking to her friend. Mom looked tired but relieved. I knew this was the right thing to do, even though it was scary. As we went inside, I felt a sense of hope. Maybe things could get better now. Maybe we would find some peace and happiness away from Nick.

That night, as I lay in the unfamiliar bed, I thought about everything that had happened. I missed my own bed and my toys, but I didn't miss the yelling and the nonstop fear. I felt safe here, surrounded by friends. I hoped that this could be the start of something happier for us.

I closed my eyes and drifted off to sleep, not sure what to think.

CHAPTER 6

My Favorite Show

1st Grade

"No more kids in my class. No damn way. I can't fit another kid in there! Hell no!"

The older woman's veins popped out along her forehead from ear to ear. On both sides! This was the first time I had ever seen that. When my mom got angry like that, no veins ever popped out.

I was worried that she was hurting her head.

My mom was oddly calm. She wasn't yelling or fighting the woman at all. Unusual. They were both looking at a man in glasses. *He's the boss*, I thought. He stared at the woman, not saying anything.

"I already have 32 kids, Bill. You told me no more at 30. I'm way over. You try managing 32 six-year-olds! I am not doing 33! Not! I don't care what you tell me!"

He stared at her, not responding. It was like a staring contest but with words. *I want to try that*, I thought to myself.

"I'll quit. I don't give a shit what you tell me. I can't and I won't," she said.

She looked tired. I felt sad for her. I thought she meant it, but I couldn't tell.

I liked that she was cursing in front of me. Only my mom cursed, and hardly ever.

Sometimes my grandparents cursed, but always in Italian.

I tried with all my might not to smile. I wanted her to curse more to see if Bill would react!

She stopped talking and stared at Bill. He stared back.

"I'll let you know tomorrow," he said.

I was surprised he spoke! It felt like Bill didn't care what she said. Not one more kid in her class, she had said. But the next morning, somehow, I was in her class, much to my surprise. I don't know what happened between her and Bill.

My mom walked me to school from Aunt May and Uncle Bernie's house in Queens. My mom and Nick were separating and needed some space. So, we were at their house for a while, Mom said.

We talked on the way in about how this new scene in Queens would be good for us and how she needed to figure things out. I told her I was glad that she and Nick were taking some time away from each other because it was getting scary at home.

She apologized for that and said she agreed. The rest of the walk to school was all about our new life in Queens and how we would adjust to living at Aunt May and Uncle Bernie's house. I told her I liked it because it was full of carpet, love, and warmth and it just felt like home.

I also feel super safe there, I thought.

She said Robert would be starting school the next day and that everything was figured out. I thought we were going back in to argue more with Bill about what to do with me, so I was surprised that when we got to school, she handed me off to someone who then took me to Mrs. Schwarmer's class.

As soon as I walked in, I felt the tension from the previous day evaporate. Mrs. Schwarmer, who had been so angry and intense the day before, was now kind and gentle.

She smiled at me, a real, warm smile that made me feel less nervous.

"Hello, Anthony," she said, kneeling down to my level. "I'm Mrs. Schwarmer. Welcome to our class."

"Hi," I mumbled, still unsure of how to react to this sudden change in her demeanor.

She must've felt sorry for me because before I knew it, I was sitting on her lap, reading my favorite book to the class. And that was only after an hour of being in her class. It felt nice, like she genuinely cared.

"Do you like reading, Anthony?" she asked me after I finished the story.

I nodded. "Yeah, a lot. My favorite book is *Where the Wild Things Are*. I just love it," I told her.

"And do you have a favorite show, Anthony?"

"My favorite show is *The Magic Garden*. I love the peaceful ladies on the swings," I said.

Her eyes lit up. "Oh, that's wonderful! Maybe we can watch it together sometime."

The next day, I gathered up the courage to remind her about the show. "Um, Mrs. Schwarmer, *The Magic Garden* is on after lunch today."

To my surprise, she smiled and said, "Really? Well, we can't miss that, can we?"

At lunch/recess, someone brought in a TV, and we all watched *The Magic Garden* together. I was so happy and felt special that she did that just for me.

As the days went by, I started to feel more and more comfortable in her class. Mrs. Schwarmer was always so patient with me, even when I was struggling. She took extra time to help me with my reading and math, always with a smile and encouraging words.

"You're doing great, Anthony," she would say. "Keep up the good work!"

One day, after a particularly good spelling test, she patted me on the back and said, "I'm so proud of you! You've improved so much."

I beamed with pride. It felt so good to be praised, especially by her. I started to excel in her class, and it was a pleasure being there for the rest of the year.

Our relationship continued to grow. She was always there to listen if I had a problem or if I was feeling sad about my parents. One day, I even felt comfortable enough to tell her about the separation.

"Mrs. Schwarmer, my mom and Nick are . . . taking a break," I said hesitantly, not sure how to describe the situation.

She looked at me with understanding in her eyes. "That must be tough for you, Anthony. But remember, it's okay to feel sad or confused. If you ever want to talk, I'm here for you."

Her words made me feel so much better. It was like having another grandmother, who understood everything. She reminded me a little bit of my grandmother.

"Don't hesitate to tell me what's on your mind," she said. "Especially on the days when you don't feel like talking. Those are the days when it's good to tell me what's going on. You'd be surprised, but you might feel better after sharing with me."

One sunny afternoon during recess, I was out on the playground with my class for a game of kickball. I was super excited because I loved being the pitcher. I had just rolled the ball when it happened.

A strong kick sent the ball flying straight toward me. I barely had time to react before it smacked me right in the face.

The impact was hard. I fell to the ground, holding my face, and tears started to come because it hurt so much. Everything seemed to spin around me as I lay there, feeling stunned and hurt. The playground got really quiet, and I could hear the other kids whispering around me.

Mrs. Schwarmer was there right away, kneeling beside me. "Anthony! Are you okay?" she asked, sounding really worried as she gently moved my hands away to see if I was hurt badly.

I tried to say something but could only nod. I could see she was worried, and that made me feel a little better, knowing she was there.

"Someone go get Anthony's mom, Jackie! Quick!" Mrs. Schwarmer called out.

"She works in the school library. You'll see her at the reference desk."

A couple of kids ran toward the school.

She looked back at me and spoke softly, "You're going to be okay, Anthony. It was just a little accident. That must have been a strong kick, huh?" She smiled at me, trying to make me feel less scared.

Soon, my mom came running over, looking really worried.

"Anthony, honey, are you all right?" she asked, kneeling beside me and gently brushing my hair from my forehead.

I tried to stop crying and felt relieved when I saw her. "I . . . I'm okay, Mom," I said, my voice shaking.

Mom hugged me tightly. "I'm here, sweetie. Everything's going to be fine."

Mrs. Schwarmer told Mom, "He took a pretty hard hit, but I don't think it's anything serious. We just wanted to be sure."

Mom smiled at her. "Thank you so much for being here with him." She looked at me, still holding my face. "How about we go inside and get some ice on that, okay?"

I nodded, feeling a little better with Mom and Mrs. Schwarmer there. As they helped me stand up, the other kids started clapping and cheering. "You'll be okay, Anthony!" one of them shouted.

"You have a strong face," another kid joked.

I couldn't help but smile a little, even though it still hurt. It felt nice to have everyone supporting me.

As we walked back inside, I held Mom's hand tightly. I was still a bit scared from what had happened, but having Mom and Mrs. Schwarmer with me made me feel safe.

The rest of the day was quiet, and I rested while my classmates were extra nice to me. Later, when we were leaving the school, Mom gave me a kiss on the forehead.

"You were so brave today, Anthony. I'm proud of you."

I smiled up at her, feeling warm and grateful. "Thanks, Mom. And thanks for coming to help."

Mom hugged me close. "Of course, sweetie. I'm here when you need me."

As we walked home, I felt safe and loved. Even though it was scary, I knew I had people who cared about me, and that made me feel better.

Another time, on a rainy afternoon, Mrs. Schwarmer told us we would be doing a special art project. She said we were going to make a "feelings collage" to show our emotions with colors and pictures. When she gave out the supplies, she noticed me sitting quietly, thinking hard.

"Anthony, would you like some help getting started?" she asked, kneeling beside my desk.

I nodded. "I don't know what to put," I said softly.

Mrs. Schwarmer smiled. "That's okay. Sometimes it's hard to know how we feel.

How about we start with colors? What color makes you feel happy?"

I thought for a moment. "Yellow," I said, thinking of the sun and the sunny days I loved.

"Great choice," she said. "And what about a color for when you're feeling a little down?"

"Maybe blue," I replied, thinking of rainy days that made me feel sad.

As we worked together, she helped me think about different ways to show my feelings. She told me it was okay to think about all my feelings, even when things were tough, like with my parents' separation.

"Remember, Anthony, it's okay to have all kinds of feelings," she said. "This collage is a safe place to show them. No feeling is too small or too big to share."

I nodded, feeling a bit more comfortable. I started cutting out pictures and words from magazines, choosing them carefully. As I glued them on the paper, I talked to her about why I picked them. We laughed when I found a picture of a funny dog that reminded me of fun times at home. I also added a picture of a cozy house because I loved staying at Aunt May and Uncle Bernie's house. It felt safe and warm there.

When I hesitated to add a picture of a stormy sea, Mrs. Schwarmer encouraged me. "It's okay to put that there, Anthony. Storms are a part of life, and they pass. Just like feelings, they come and go."

With her help, I added the picture and felt a bit better. Sharing my feelings on the collage made me feel like a weight was lifted off my shoulders.

As we finished the project, Mrs. Schwarmer kept checking in with me, giving me support and letting me express myself. She told me how proud she was of my collage and how it showed my feelings and experiences.

On the day we shared our collages, Mrs. Schwarmer stood beside me as I presented mine to the class. I felt nervous but also proud of what I had made. As I talked about the pictures and colors I chose, I felt a connection with my classmates and gratitude for Mrs. Schwarmer's support.

Afterward, she gave me a big hug. "You did an amazing job, Anthony. I'm so proud of you for sharing your feelings with us."

I felt so happy at that moment. Mrs. Schwarmer made me feel understood. She wasn't just my teacher; she cared about me and helped me feel confident in expressing myself. Her kindness made me feel special and encouraged.

As the school year continued, I grew closer to her and to my classmates. We did fun projects, learned new things, and even had a little party on the last day of school. I felt like I belonged, like I was part of something special.

On the last day, as we said goodbye, Mrs. Schwarmer hugged me and said,

"Anthony, you've been such a joy to have in class. I'm going to miss you."

I hugged her back, tears in my eyes. "I'll miss you too, Mrs. Schwarmer. Thank you for everything."

I was so glad Mrs. Schwarmer believed in me. I knew I would remember her forever.

As I walked out of the classroom for the last time, I felt a mix of emotions, sad, happy, and a little scared about what was next.

CHAPTER 7

Hubba! Hubba! Hubba!

1st Grade

"THAT *SESAME STREET* SONG WITH THE CLOWN," ROBERT SAID.

"1-2-3-4-5-6-7-8, penny candy man," I sang, as Robert and I walked along the city street after school in Queens, New York.

"Eight cents buys eight valentine hearts . . . Hubba, hubba, hubba," he said.

"I can't get it out of my head," I said, skipping and walking.

We both sang, "Hubba, hubba, hubba . . . Hubba, hubba, hubba, hubba, hubba."

"It's stuck in my head, Rob," I laughed. "I can't get it out."

"Why get it out?" he said. "Just go with it."

As the afternoon light began to wane, Robert and I made our way home, still singing the *Sesame Street* song. We laughed and sang the whole way.

"Hubba, hubba, hubba . . . Hubba, hubba, hubba, hubba, hubba," we sang in unison as we opened the front door.

Nick was in the living room, drinking a can of Miller High Life beer and watching TV. I looked his way and liked the colors of the gold and green can he was holding. I saw that his eyes narrowed as he could hear us singing.

He had little patience for noise, especially when it came from us, his stepsons.

"Cut that racket!" he barked, his face twisting into a scowl. We kept singing and having fun.

"Did you hear me? I said, 'Shut up!'" Nick's voice boomed through the house.

With a surge of anger, he stormed over, grabbing each of us by the arm. He told us to meet him in the basement. The sound of the song was replaced by the harsh, frightening sounds of Nick's anger.

When it was over, Nick left us there, slamming the basement door behind him.

The air was thick with the echo of his rage and the pain that followed in its wake.

In the dim light of the basement of our aunt and uncle's house, my brother and I huddled together.

"Why does he get so mad, Rob?" I whispered, my voice trembling.

"I don't know," Robert said, wincing as he shifted his weight. "He just does. We can't let him get to us, though."

I nodded, trying to be brave. "At least we're here now."

"Yeah," Robert agreed. "Aunt May and Uncle Bernie will make sure we're okay."

We fell into a heavy silence. We had each other and our shared strength. We stayed in the basement, in the quiet, not knowing what to do. We played rock, paper, scissors and a number game with our fingers to pass the time without talking much.

"Let's get out of here," Robert said to me after the upstairs was quiet for almost an hour. Once we opened the door, we could see Nick passed out sleeping on the couch.

"Let's go outside and play," Robert said. I agreed. We wanted to go outside and explore Queens a little.

"Is that Billy?" Rob asked.

"Yep," I said.

Billy Battaby rode up on a brand-new, shiny orange bike.

"Whoa . . . What is that?" Rob asked.

"It's a Raleigh Chopper bicycle," Billy bragged. "I just got it for my birthday from my rich uncle."

"I wish I had that bike," Rob said.

"Me too," I said with a sigh.

"There's no way I'll ever get a bike like that," I whispered to my brother.

"I wish we had a rich uncle," Rob whispered back.

Rob said loudly, "Our mom says we can't get bikes while we're here because we're not staying too long now that our dad, Nick, is visiting. We're going home soon."

"Are we really going home soon?" I whispered to Rob. He didn't answer.

"You'll never get a bike like this," Billy said to my brother. "Your parents hate each other, and they can't afford this bike anyway."

Billy was mostly a mean kid. We had met him during a snowball fight, and he was mean to us for a long time after we arrived in Queens.

Rob didn't care that Billy was mean. And one day, they became friends. Now we played outside together all the time.

"We shouldn't even hang out with you guys because you're not staying," Billy said as he stared at Rob and me. "But there's not too many kids around here."

Our friend Tommy yelled from down the street, shouting over his loud black Big Wheel tires.

"I saw you guys and I told my mom I was coming out," Tommy said. "I ran out before she could tell me no, so I may not be out here long."

My mom called Tommy a "troublemaker." She wasn't wrong. He had once talked me into sitting in the swooped handlebars of his Spyder bike to ride to school faster. We were late. He rode off the sidewalk into the dirt, and I flew off the handlebars onto the street—headfirst. Lots of blood and tears. I still have the bump, right in the center of my forehead.

It was like a scene from *The Three Stooges*, I had thought to myself as I made my way to school.

When I got there, people's eyes bugged out like I had never seen. I thought my mom was going to kill me when she found out I was riding on the handlebars, but she just yelled a lot as she dragged me to the nurse's office as fast as she could. I could tell she was worried.

I got in trouble for riding on Tommy's bike, but my mom let us play with the kids in the neighborhood because we had so much more fun with them than we did in our neighborhood in Florida, where it was mostly old people who were retired living there.

Our days in Queens seemed to stretch on forever, filled with endless adventures. Robert and I quickly found ourselves part of the lively neighborhood scene. The kids there were always ready for the next big adventure, and having us join the gang brought something new and exciting.

One sunny afternoon, after finishing our morning chores, Robert and I met up with Billy and Tommy in the park. The park was our favorite spot, a big green place surrounded by tall buildings where we could forget all our worries and just be kids.

"Let's build a fort," Tommy said, his eyes twinkling with excitement.

"Yeah, over in those trees," Billy added, pointing to a small cluster of trees at the edge of the park.

We got to work right away, gathering branches, leaves, and anything else we could find. Everyone pitched in. Even Billy seemed happy to be part of the group.

"Look at this branch," I said, holding up a big sturdy piece of wood. "We can use it as the main support."

"Great find," Robert said, helping me drag the branch over to our fort.

We laughed and talked as we built, sharing stories and jokes. The fort slowly came together, a symbol of our friendship and teamwork. When we finally finished, we stood back to admire what we had made.

"It's perfect," Tommy said proudly.

"We should have a secret password to get in," Billy suggested.

"How about 'Hubba, hubba, hubba?'" I said with a big grin.

"Perfect," Robert agreed. "'Hubba, hubba, hubba' it is."

The fort became our headquarters, a place to plan our next adventures and escape from the world. We spent countless hours there, playing games, telling ghost stories, and just enjoying being together.

One day, while hanging out in the fort, we heard a commotion on the other side of the park. Curious, we went to check it out and found a group of older kids bullying a younger boy.

"Hey, leave him alone!" Robert shouted, stepping forward bravely.

The older kids turned to us, sneering. "Or what?" one of them taunted.

"Or we'll make you," Billy said, surprising everyone with his boldness.

The standoff didn't last long. The older kids saw the determination in our eyes and decided it wasn't worth the trouble. They left, and the younger boy, who was named Jimmy, thanked us over and over.

"You guys are awesome," Jimmy said, looking up at us with wide eyes.

"Stick with us, and you'll be safe," I said, patting Jimmy on the back.

Jimmy quickly became part of our group, and our bond grew even stronger. We kept exploring the neighborhood, finding new and exciting places to play and challenges to tackle.

One of our favorite things to do was play baseball in the empty lot down the street. We formed teams and had epic games that sometimes lasted all day. Robert and I discovered we were pretty good at the game, with Robert being a strong hitter and me being a fast runner.

"You're like the dynamic duo," Tommy said one day after a particularly intense game.

"Maybe we'll be famous baseball players one day," Robert said, smiling.

"Yeah, and we'll buy our own Raleigh Chopper bikes," I added with a laugh.

Our days were filled with adventures. Even though we missed our mom during the day, we had happiness and comfort in our little group, knowing we had each other.

The days of adventure couldn't last forever, though. One evening, as we were returning home, we found Nick waiting for us on the porch. His face was twisted in anger, and the sight of him made our hearts sink.

"Where have you two been?" he demanded.

"We were just playing at the park," Robert replied, trying to keep his voice steady.

"'Playing at the park,'" Nick mocked, his voice dripping with disdain. "You think you can just do whatever you want? Your mother is worried sick, and you two are out having fun."

"We didn't mean to worry her," I said, feeling a knot tighten in my stomach.

"Didn't mean to?" Nick's voice rose. "You're both a couple of selfish brats. Get inside, now!"

We hurried past him, the joy of the day draining away. Inside, we found our mom sitting on the couch, looking tired and stressed. She glanced at us with sad eyes, but Nick's presence kept her silent.

Every little thing set him off, and we could never predict what would trigger his anger. The tension in the house was palpable, a constant weight on our shoulders.

Aunt May and Uncle Bernie had gone to visit friends for the weekend and left us alone. I think they were hoping this would give Mom and Nick a chance to repair their marriage.

It wasn't working.

The next night was a bad one. Nick erupted over something minor. His shouting echoed through the house, and he lashed out and hit us. It was clear he had no intention of changing, and his anger would always find a way to surface.

After he stormed out, slamming the door behind him, we sat in silence, the air thick with the aftermath of his rage. Our mom looked at us, her eyes filled with sorrow and resignation.

"I'm sorry, boys," she said softly. "I thought things would get better, but I see now that they won't. He's leaving tomorrow. We'll stay here with Aunt May and Uncle Bernie."

Relief washed over us, mixed with sadness for our mom. We knew she was making the right choice, but it didn't make it any easier for her. You could see it in her face.

The next morning, Nick had his suitcase and left the house that had become a battleground. I watched him scowl at us from the back seat of the taxi car as it drove away.

We are better off without him, I thought.

In the days that followed, we found a new place to call home. It wasn't always easy, but without Nick's anger hanging over us, we began to relax. Our mom found her smile again, and we discovered that life could be full of joy and adventure once more.

Aunt May and Uncle Bernie knew how to have fun with us. They kept our minds off of the trouble going on with Nick and Mom. Aunt May is the world's best cook. And Uncle Bernie makes the best peanut butter and jelly sandwiches.

Robert and I continued to play with our friends, build forts, and dream of Raleigh Chopper bikes.

We knew from mom that we were only here for a few months before we went back to Florida. We made the most of it. It felt safe to be around family here and I was surprised how quickly it felt like home.

CHAPTER 8

Under the Bed

2nd Grade

I ALWAYS THOUGHT THE HULK WAS THE COOLEST. GREEN, STRONG, and brave.

Not like me. I was just eight years old, and I couldn't even protect my family.

Not like the Hulk.

I really wished I could turn into him, especially when Nick showed up. He was like the meanest villain ever. In the most recent issue, the Abomination was the Hulk's enemy, and he was the meanest, angriest villain I'd ever seen in a Hulk comic.

I had even been having nightmares about him. The night before, I had woken up from a dream, feeling the pointer finger on his right hand pushing into my right leg, just above my knee. I could feel it! It woke me up and I thought he was there, in my room at the foot of my bed.

Nick was the Abomination. He was mean. Really mean. He hurt my mom and yelled a lot. Mom told us to hide under the bed when he came over. He smelled like alcohol. I could smell him from two rooms away.

There we were again, under the bed.

The floor was cold under Robert's bed. His bed was the furthest from the door, so it was the safest place to hide. I was lying closest to the door, looking out. I told Rob I wanted to be the lookout guy. He was next to the wall, and our little sister, Donna, was between us. She had just had her fifth birthday, and her wish was to never see Nick again.

He wanted to take her from us. He kept telling Mom that. Mom said he never would, that it would be over her dead body.

I hoped that wouldn't happen.

"Open the door, Jackie! I know you're in there!" Nick's voice boomed through the house. He was pounding on the door with his gun again. I could hear the heavy thuds and the way the door rattled in its frame. Each thud made my heart jump. I wished I had my Hulk figurine with me. I had left him in the living room, and now it was too late to get him.

No way I was going in there.

Unless I had to.

Mom's voice was shaky. "Nick, please go away. The kids are scared. You need to leave."

"I ain't leaving without Donna!" Nick screamed back. "You hear me? I'll shoot this door down if I have to!"

Robert's eyes were big and scared. He whispered to Donna, "Don't worry, we're not gonna let him take you."

Donna was crying softly, and I tried to be brave for her. "Yeah, Donna, we're here to protect you." I reached out and held her little hand. She was trembling.

"Open up, Jackie! Last chance!" Nick's voice was louder now, and the gun banged harder against the door. I could feel each bang in my chest, like the Abomination was smashing something. But it wasn't the Abomination. It was Nick. He was bad.

Mom finally opened the door. I heard the creak and Nick's heavy footsteps as he pushed his way in.

"You think you can keep me out of my own house?" he yelled.

"This isn't your house anymore, Nick," Mom said. She had kicked him out. Her voice was strong now, but I knew she was scared. "You need to leave. You're not taking Donna. Go back to your hotel!"

Nick laughed. It was a mean laugh. Some of his words were slurring.

"Oh, really? And who's gonna stop me? You? You can't stop me, Jackie. If we're separating, I get my daughter."

"Over my dead body," Mom said. She was standing firm, even with Nick waving his gun around.

It was just like the time the cop pulled us over on 441. She had been fearless with the officer and yelled at him for pulling us over. I thought he was gonna arrest her, but he didn't. She was tough!

I was worried she was being too tough now. *Maybe I should go out there and try to reason with them somehow*, I thought to myself.

"Yeah? Well, that can be arranged," Nick said, stepping closer to her. "I'm taking her, and there's nothing you can do about it."

"You are not taking Donna!" Mom screamed back. "She's my daughter too, and I won't let you near her. You're drunk and dangerous!"

"You watch your mouth, Jackie," Nick snarled. "You don't get to decide anything anymore. I'm her father!"

"You lost that right the moment you started waving that gun around," Mom shouted. "You're not fit to be around any of us!"

The yelling got louder, and I heard a crash. I flinched, and Donna clung to me.

"What's happening?" she asked, her voice full of fear.

"I don't know," I said. "But it's gonna be okay. We'll be okay."

I wished I could believe it. I wished I could be the Hulk. But all we could do was hold each other and hope Mom would be okay. That we would all be okay.

Then, suddenly, there was a new sound. A loud banging on the door.

"This is the police! Open up!"

Nick's voice dropped, but it was still angry. "What the hell? Who called the cops?"

Mom's voice was shaky again. "I'm sure it was our neighbors across the street, Burt and Jack, Nick. They look out for us. You need to leave."

"I ain't leaving," Nick yelled. "I got rights."

"They offered to move the kids and me into their house to protect us," she said. "That's how bad this is. That's how out of control this has become. Are you proud of yourself? Your family has to move across the street to stay safe from you!"

"You'll never leave this house!" Nick yelled.

The police kept banging. "Sir, you need to open the door. We just want to talk."

Nick didn't move at first, but then there was more banging. "Fine!" he shouted, and I heard him stomp to the door and yank it open. "What do you want?"

"Sir, we need you to calm down and step outside," one of the officers said. "We got a call about a disturbance."

"This is my house!" Nick yelled. "You can't make me leave!"

"Sir, we just want to talk. Can you step outside, please?"

There was a pause, and then I heard Nick step outside, still grumbling. The door closed, and I could hear muffled voices. I couldn't make out what they were saying, but it didn't sound good.

Mom's voice was closer now. She must have moved to the hallway. "Kids, stay under the bed. Don't come out until I say so."

Robert's eyes were wide and scared. Donna was still crying softly. I held them both tight, trying to be brave.

"Robert," I whispered, "do you think Mom will be okay?"

Robert's voice was just as shaky as mine. "I hope so, Anthony. But we have to stay here like Mom said. We can't help it if we get hurt too."

I squeezed Donna's hand. "Donna, don't worry. We're here to protect you."

Donna sniffled, her tiny voice shaking. "I don't want him to take me. I wanna stay with you guys."

"You will," Robert assured her. "We're not letting him take you. Right, Anthony?"

"Right," I said firmly. "We'll protect you, Donna. We're here for you."

The talking outside got louder again. "Nick, you need to leave and cool off," one of the officers said.

"I ain't going nowhere!" Nick shouted. "This is my house, and you can't make me leave!"

"Sir, we're not trying to arrest you. We just want you to leave and cool off for a while. Can you do that?"

"No! I ain't going anywhere! You can't make me!"

"Mr. Squicciarini, we understand this is difficult, but you're causing a scene. For everyone's safety, we need you to leave and calm down," the officer insisted.

"You don't understand anything!" Nick bellowed. "This is my family, and I have every right to be here!"

"Calm down," said a voice, which sounded like our neighbor Burt. His voice was steady and calm. "Think about the kids. They need to feel safe."

"Yeah, Nick," Jack said. Our neighbor had come over from across the street.

"Just take a walk, cool off. This isn't helping anyone."

"I don't need you two telling me what to do!" Nick snapped. "I can handle my own family!"

"Nick, please," Mom's voice was back, soft and pleading. "Just go. We can talk about this later. Please, for the kids."

"Nick, you don't want to do this," Burt, Jack's wife, said, trying to keep the peace.

"Think about your daughter, man. She needs her dad to be calm and rational."

"Rational? You don't know what you're talking about, Burt!" Nick spat. "This is my family, and I'll handle it how I see fit."

"Nick, you're scaring everyone," Jack chimed in, trying to reason with him.

"Please, just listen to reason."

"I ain't leaving! You hear me?" Nick's voice was loud and angry. "Jackie, you better tell them to back off. This is my house!"

"Nick, for God's sake, just go," Mom's voice was breaking. "Think about Donna. Think about the kids."

"You think I don't care about my daughter?" Nick shouted. "She's mine, Jackie. You can't keep her from me."

Donna sniffled, her tiny voice shaking. "I don't want him to take me. I wanna stay with you guys."

"You will," Robert assured her. "We're not letting him take you."

The tension was thick in the air, and my heart was pounding so hard I thought it might burst. Finally, I heard Nick's footsteps moving away. "Fine," he muttered. "But this ain't over."

A door slammed.

There was a long silence.

I listened closely. I heard a car door open and close loudly. That was him. *He's so loud*, I thought.

Then I heard the sound of tires moving and shooting up dirt and pebbles. The engine accelerated. I knew that sound clearly— his car was driving away. I could hear it. I could feel it in my heart.

Another long silence.

I wondered why it was so quiet. What was everyone doing? Was no one moving?

Suddenly, the silence broke. I heard what sounded like my mom's footsteps, walking toward us. We all remained frozen under the bed. It was like time was standing still for me.

Mom broke the silence with her words.

"Kids, you can come out now. It's okay."

We crawled out from under the bed, and Mom hugged us tight. "It's gonna be okay," she whispered. "We're safe now."

"But Mom, what if he comes back?" Robert asked, his voice shaky.

"He won't come back tonight," Mom reassured him, stroking his hair. "The police are going to make sure of that. We have Burt and Jack looking out for us too."

Donna clung to Mom's leg. "I don't want him to come back ever," she said, her voice low and frightened.

"I know, sweetheart," Mom said, kneeling down to her level. "We're going to make sure he can't hurt us anymore. We're going to be okay."

I looked up at Mom, my own fear still lingering. "Mom, what if he tries to take Donna again? Are we safe in our home? Can the North Lauderdale police protect us?"

Mom sighed and hugged me tighter. "We'll make sure he can't. We'll talk to the police and get help. You don't have to worry about that. Right now, we need to stay together and stay strong."

Robert nodded, taking a deep breath. "Mom, are you okay?"

Mom smiled, though it was a tired smile. "I'm okay, Robert. I'm just glad you guys are safe. That's what matters most."

Donna looked up at Mom with wide eyes. "Can we sleep in your room tonight?"

"Of course you can," Mom said softly. "We'll all stay together tonight. I think we all need that."

As we walked to Mom's room, I could feel the tension slowly easing. The fear was still there, but we were together. Mom made sure we felt safe, and her calm words helped me believe that we really would be okay.

When we settled into Mom's bed, Robert whispered to me, "Do you think we'll really be safe?"

I nodded, even though I wasn't entirely sure. "Yeah, I think so. Mom's tough. She won't let anything happen to us."

Donna snuggled between us, holding onto Mom's hand. "I love you, Mom."

"I love you too, Donna," Mom said, kissing her forehead. "I love all of you. We're going to be okay. I promise."

As I lay there, feeling the warmth of my family around me, I started to believe it. The fear wasn't completely gone, but for the first time in a while, I felt a glimmer of hope. Maybe we could be okay. Maybe we could be safe.

And that was enough for now.

CHAPTER 9

A Safe Haven

2nd Grade

THE NEXT DAY, I WAS SO GLAD TO GO TO MISS SCHROEDER'S CLASS. I woke up and started to get dressed.

I loved listening to the radio when I got dressed. I opened my drawer and was proud that I knew how to match my clothes. My mom would brag to people about my clothes-matching ability. I would typically listen to the news while getting dressed in the morning, but today I knew the news wasn't what I wanted. I needed to feel happy. Music made me happy.

"This is W-A-X-Y, WAXY 106. Greg Budell here. Good morning, everyone!" radio host Budell blared out.

The song started.

"106, WAXY FM . . . Here's a recent hit and request for you—'Midnight at the Oasis' by Maria Muldaur."

"Midnight at the oasis. Send your camel to bed. Shadows painting our faces.

Traces of romance in our heads . . . "

While listening, I realized that Miss Schroeder's class felt like an oasis.

My mom's brother, Uncle Jerry, would say I had an old soul because I was wise beyond my years. I didn't know how I could be that, but I knew I felt what he meant when I listened to the music on WAXY 106.

As I walked to school with Robert that day, the song kept running through my head.

"WAXY 106 is my favorite radio station," I told him. "I can hear the songs in my head whenever I want."

"Me too," Rob said. "Sometimes I can't make them stop playing."

We both laughed. We hardly spoke after that as we walked. The heaviness of yesterday with Nick and Mom and us under the bed seemed to follow us to school.

School was my favorite place to be. I felt safe and happy there, away from the chaos at home.

At school, everything was different, especially in Miss Schroeder's classroom.

Miss Schroeder's room was bright and colorful. There were posters of the alphabet, numbers, and animals on the walls. The back of the room had a relaxing reading library with beanbags and a small carpet. It was my favorite spot. The desks were arranged in neat rows, and my name was written in perfect cursive on a tag on my desk.

Miss Schroeder was different from other teachers. She was around my mom's age, I guessed. Sometimes she seemed distant, like she was thinking about something far away. She had kind eyes, and I felt safe when she looked at me. Her desk at the front of the room was always messy with papers, books, and her coffee mug. She seemed tired, yet she always had time for me.

When I walked into Miss Schroeder's classroom, the familiar warmth and safety washed over me. The smell of her coffee and the faint scent of chalk welcomed me like a comforting hug.

"Good morning, Anthony!" Miss Schroeder greeted me with a bright smile. "How are you today?"

"I was listening to WAXY 106 this morning," I said. "I don't know why in second grade I would like oldies, but I like oldies!"

"It's because that was the best music," she said with a smile. "Much better than today's music."

"I don't mind top 40 music," I said. "I do like Y100 for the top 40 countdown. Otherwise, it's oldies and the Beatles for me."

She stared at me, her eyebrows and forehead wrinkled.

"You seem off today," she said with a higher voice than usual. "How are you really?"

I hesitated for a moment. My stomach dropped. How did she know?!

I decided to tell her a little.

"I'm okay," I said quietly, looking down at my shoes. "Just a little tired."

Miss Schroeder's eyes softened. She walked over and knelt down beside me. "Did you have trouble sleeping last night?" she asked gently.

I nodded, not wanting to say more. But Miss Schroeder always seemed to understand without me having to explain.

"Why don't you come over to the reading corner for a bit?" she suggested. "You can pick out a book and get comfortable."

I nodded again and made my way to the cozy reading corner. I picked out a book about reptiles, one of my favorites. I loved dinosaurs. I then settled into a beanbag. Miss Schroeder followed me and sat down in the chair next to me.

"Do you want to talk about it?" she asked softly. "Sometimes it helps to share what's on your mind."

I looked up at her, feeling the weight of yesterday's events pressing down on me.

"My dad Nick was really angry yesterday," I said, my voice barely above a whisper. "He yelled at Mom, and we had to hide under the bed."

Miss Schroeder reached out and gently squeezed my hand. "I'm so sorry, Anthony," she said. "That sounds really scary. But you know what? You're very brave. And I'm so glad you're here today."

Her words made me feel a little better. I took a deep breath and tried to focus on the book in my hands. "I see you like reptiles," she said.

"Do you like animals, Miss Schroeder?" I asked, wanting to change the subject to something happier.

"I do," she replied, smiling. "I used to have a dog named Max. He was the sweetest dog in the world. Do you have any pets?"

I shook my head. "No, but I wish I did. I like dogs, too."

"Did your family ever have a dog?" she asked.

"Yes, we had a dog named Snoopy," I said, smiling. "He was as tall as me and would pounce on people when they came to the door. His tongue would hang out of his mouth. He was so fun!"

"Where is he now?" she asked.

"When me and my brother and sister moved to Queens last year to live with my great aunt and uncle when my mom and dad broke up, Nick, took him to a farm to live with other animals," I said. "He told us he'd be happier there. I miss him. He always put me in a good mood!"

"My aunt and uncle helped raise our mom when she was a little girl, so we were so lucky we had their house to go to in Queens, Mom says," I told Miss Schroeder. "We paid a price to go to New York by losing Snoopy in Florida because of Nick."

Miss Schroeder leaned in a little closer. "Maybe someday you'll have another dog, or when you get older you can have a dog of your own," she said. "In the meantime, we can read all about them. How does that sound?"

"That sounds good," I said, feeling a small smile tug at my lips.

As we read together, the tension from home began to fade away. Miss Schroeder's voice was soothing, and I felt safe sitting next to her. For a little while, I could forget about the chaos at home and just be a kid enjoying a story.

After a while, the other kids started to arrive, and the classroom buzzed with the usual morning chatter. Miss Schroeder stood up and straightened her skirt. "All right, everyone," she called out. "Time to get started with our day. Let's begin with our morning meeting."

I took my seat at my desk, feeling a little more at ease. Miss Schroeder's presence always made things better, and I was grateful for the haven she provided.

Throughout the day, Miss Schroeder would glance my way and give me an encouraging smile. It was our little secret, a silent promise that everything would be okay.

And in her classroom, I believed it.

Throughout the day, I felt her comforting presence. She had a way of making everything seem brighter and more manageable. During our math lesson, I found myself drifting back to the events at home, but Miss Schroeder noticed and gently brought me back to the present.

"Anthony, can you help me pass out these worksheets?" she asked with a smile.

I nodded, grateful for the distraction. As I walked around the room, I felt a sense of responsibility that made me feel important and needed. It gave me a sense of belonging.

Later in the day, we had a writing assignment. Miss Schroeder asked us to write about our favorite place. I hesitated at first, not sure what to write about. My mind was filled with thoughts of home, but I didn't want to write about that.

Miss Schroeder walked over and knelt beside my desk again. "Having trouble getting started?" she asked softly.

I nodded. "I don't know what to write about."

"Why don't you write about a place that makes you feel happy and safe?" she suggested. "It could be real or imaginary."

I thought about her words and started to write. I wrote about a beautiful garden with flowers of every color and a big tree with a swing hanging from its branches. In my garden, there was a small pond with fish swimming lazily and birds singing in the trees. It was a place where I felt calm and happy, a place where nothing could hurt me.

When I finished, Miss Schroeder came over to read my work. "This is beautiful, Anthony," she said, her eyes soft and kind. "I can see how much you love this place."

I smiled, feeling a warmth spread through me. "Thank you, Miss Schroeder."

After lunch, we had art class. Art was one of my favorite subjects because it allowed me to express myself without words. Today, we were painting. Miss Schroeder gave us each a canvas and some paints and told us to create something that made us feel happy.

I decided to paint the garden from my story. I carefully chose bright colors for the flowers and a soft blue for the sky. As I painted, I felt the tension from home start to melt away. It was as if I was transported to my imaginary garden, and for a little while, everything was perfect. I imagined dinosaurs roaming the garden and eating the leaves.

Miss Schroeder walked around the room, admiring our work. When she reached my desk, she smiled warmly. "This is wonderful, Anthony. You have a real talent for painting."

I blushed, feeling proud of my work. "Thank you, Miss Schroeder."

As the day drew to a close, I felt a sense of calm that I hadn't felt in a long time. Miss Schroeder's classroom was my sanctuary, a place where I could be myself and feel safe.

At the end of the day, Miss Schroeder called me over to her desk. "Anthony, I want you to know that if you ever need to talk, I'm here for you," she said gently. "You can always come to me if you're feeling scared or sad."

I nodded, feeling a lump form in my throat. "Thank you, Miss Schroeder. That means a lot to me."

She gave me a reassuring smile. "You're a very special boy, Anthony. Remember that."

As I left the classroom and walked home with Robert, I felt a sense of hope. I knew that no matter what happened at home, I was safe in Miss Schroeder's class. That made all the difference.

The next day, it was a rainy afternoon. While the other kids were reading, Miss Schroeder called me to the back of the room where the reading library was. The sound of rain tapping on the windows made it feel even cozier.

"Anthony," she said softly, "I noticed you've been doing really well in class. How are things at home?"

I hesitated, my fingers picking at the edge of my book. I looked up at her, and her kind eyes made me feel a little braver. "It's still not good, Miss Schroeder. My dad, Nick, is always angry. He drinks a lot and yells at my mom, my brother, and me. He doesn't yell at my sister, thank goodness. You see he's a stepdad to me an my brother, but our sister is his, so he treats her well."

Miss Schroeder's face showed she cared. She put a hand on my shoulder. "I'm so sorry to hear that, Anthony. It must be really hard for you."

I nodded, a tear slipping down my cheek. "I don't like being at home. I'm scared all the time. But I like being here, in school. It's safe and warm."

Miss Schroeder's eyes were sad, but she smiled at me. "You know, Anthony, you can always talk to me. Whenever you need to."

I nodded again, feeling a little better. From then on, we had lots of talks. During recess or when the other kids were busy, I'd find my way to the back of the room, and Miss Schroeder would be there, ready to listen. I told her about my fears, my dreams, and my worries. And she told me about her life, too.

The next day in class, I told Miss Schroeder about my biggest fear.

"I'm scared my family will be split apart," I whispered. "I don't think my mom can handle it all. I'm worried she might have to give us up, or that Nick will hurt us more." Miss Schroeder's eyes filled with tears as she listened. She took a deep breath. "Anthony, you're very brave for sharing this with me. It's not your job to fix things at home. But it's important that you and your brother stay safe. Have you talked to anyone else about this? Maybe another adult you trust?"

I shook my head. "No one outside of my family. I feel safe talking to you."

Miss Schroeder's face softened. "Thank you for feeling that way, Anthony. I'm always here for you, and we'll figure this out together, okay?"

I nodded, feeling a sense of relief. For the first time, I felt like I wasn't alone.

I noticed that Miss Schroeder seemed to look forward to our talks, too. She'd smile more, and her eyes didn't look as tired. She told me that I helped her feel less lonely. It made me feel good to know that I was helping her, too.

"Who else can you talk with about what's happening at home, Anthony?" she asked.

"My great aunt and uncle, Aunt May and Uncle Bernie, just moved nearby to Margate to be there for us, they said," I told her. "They raised my mom. And we stayed with them last year. They're here to help."

"Anyone else you can talk to?"

"My Uncle Jerry," I said. "He's my mom's brother. He's so cool. He has long curly hair, and my mom says he was a hippie in the 60s. He only visits every now and then, but when he comes, it's so much fun. He makes ice cream sundaes, and we go for drives.

Sometimes just the two of us will drive and talk."

"That's so good that you can talk with him," she said.

"He calls me an old soul," I said. "He told me to be there for my mom because she's going through a hard time in her life, but things will be okay soon."

"Is he married?" she asked.

"No," I said.

"I'll be like your aunt then," she said. "You ARE an old soul. He's right. Sometimes you give me advice and notice things about my life that even I don't perceive."

That made me feel really good. I felt like Superman walking out of school that day.

One afternoon, near the end of the school year, I gave Miss Schroeder a letter. I had written it carefully, wanting her to know how much she meant to me.

"Miss Schroeder, I wrote you a letter," I said, handing it to her.

She unfolded the paper and read it. I wrote about how much her kindness and support meant to me, and how she made me feel safe and valued.

Miss Schroeder had tears in her eyes as she read my words. She looked up at me, her voice shaky. "Thank you, Anthony. This means so much to me. You've been so strong, and I'm so proud of you."

I smiled, feeling proud. For the first time, I felt like my voice mattered.

For the first time in my life, I was looking forward to the summer and the next school year.

I felt like life was getting better. The bond I shared with Miss Schroeder had given me the strength. I was sad to leave her classroom at the end of the year, but I knew I was stronger because of her.

I cried on our last day of school that year. She did too.

"Miss Schroeder, I feel more like Superman and less like the Hulk," I said. "I don't even like Superman comics. They're kind of boring. The villains aren't that good.

The villains in the Hulk, they really bring it!"

Years later, I often thought about Miss Schroeder and the time I spent in her classroom. She had shown me kindness and understanding during a very hard time in my life. As I grew older, I remembered the lessons she taught me about trust, resilience, and the power of a caring heart.

I hoped that Miss Schroeder retired from teaching with a heart full of memories, knowing she had made a difference in her students' lives. She is a testament to the power of compassion, understanding, and the bonds that can be formed between a teacher and a student.

CHAPTER 10

The Triplex

2nd Grade

It was the summer between second and third grade.

My mom had a date with a guy named Vito, who it turned out was her divorce attorney. They were going on a double date with Mom's best friend, Lori, and Lori's boyfriend.

Lori had two kids, Diane and Stacey. We hung out with them a lot. My brother and sister and I always got excited if we knew we were going to see them. Since our moms often spent time together, we'd been seeing them more.

The plan was for all of us to hang out at Lori's place, in part because Nick didn't know where Lori lived. So, my mom knew that if she dropped us off there to go out on a date, Nick wouldn't come looking for us there. We were doing everything we could to not be home as much as possible because Nick was spying on us. My mom called him a stalker. I didn't know what she meant. I just knew it was bad. He was bad.

Lori came to our house, and we all got in her car, including my mom. Then Lori drove us to her place. The plan was to throw Nick off because my mom's car would still be in our driveway, and he might drive by and assume we were home. If he was in a really foul mood and tried to bang the door down or threaten us, no one would be home.

"Hopefully he doesn't break into his own house only to find out we're not there," Mom told Lori.

They both laughed. Rob and Donna and I were in the back seat. I wasn't laughing and neither were they.

We smiled some though because we knew we were about to see our friends. We talked about what we were going to do once we got there. The car ride went by quickly, as we were all so excited.

Lori lived in a triplex, which I had never seen before. It was like one long curved house broken up into three houses, but they were all attached. My mom said they called them triplexes or attached houses. I said they looked like large apartments with only one floor. Some of my friends lived in apartment buildings near my elementary school. They were built really close to the 7-Eleven near there.

We pulled into a circular driveway in front of the middle house, or apartment, as I was calling it.

As we got out of the car, I noticed an older, pretty woman with blonde hair and her husband. I thought they must live in the house on the left because they were standing in front of it, checking the mailbox.

The third apartment of the triplex was a mystery. I couldn't see who lived there. It looked like no one was home.

Our mom and Lori walked us inside and said hi to the girls. They squealed when we came in, and they ran around telling us all about their living room and all the toys that we could play with, like Diane's Barbie dolls. She had so many of them!

We all hung out, eating pizza that Lori cooked in the oven for us and Lay's potato chips and drinking Pepsi. Eventually, Lori's boyfriend came by and spent some time with us. Robert and I went outside and played catch using a football and then a frisbee.

Soon, Vito came over. My mom introduced Robert, Donna, and I to him. He was about the same height as my mom. He had a very bushy face. Lots of hair everywhere. A beard, a mustache, and a big thick head of black hair. You could hardly see his face with all that hair. He did have a big smile though and what looked to be kind eyes. I liked the way he looked at my mom. He admired her when she spoke, and she smiled at him when he looked at her like that.

After dinner, as the four adults left, Mom said Robert was in charge, since he was the oldest.

We hugged our mom goodbye and waved at the guys as they walked out last.

"Have fun at dinner!" Robert called as the car pulled away. He had stepped just outside the front door to say goodbye and then came back in.

"We'll watch cartoons, maybe a movie, and play games."

Soon the house filled with the sounds of laughter and cartoons. We talked about what to watch on TV and shared all about the shows we liked to watch. I told the girls I loved *Popeye* and watched all of the episodes, even the old black-and-white ones.

The girls said they watched *The Muppet Show* and *Land of the Lost*. We all agreed that those were our new favorite shows.

About ten minutes later, not long after the adults drove off, the phone rang. Robert hesitated and looked at me. I shrugged. He then picked it up.

"Hello?" Robert said cautiously.

"Hello, who is this?" a man's voice asked sharply.

"This is Robert. Who's this?" Robert responded.

"Robert who?" the man's voice grew angrier. I could hear the man's voice getting louder.

"Robert Squicciarini," Robert said.

"Robert Squicciarini?!" the man yelled.

The voice was unmistakable. It was Nick, and he sounded furious. I could hear that it was him. I felt like I might poop my pants.

"How did he get this number?" I said out loud in frustration.

"I'll be right over!" Nick shouted before Robert could react.

Robert hung up the phone immediately.

"Oh no! Everyone, Nick is coming!" I exclaimed, panic setting in. "He's coming here!"

The girls started running around, screaming. Everyone was afraid of Nick, and we all worried he would take Donna if there were no adults around to stop him.

"Robert, what are we going to do?" I asked, my voice trembling. My breathing was fast.

"I don't know," Robert replied. He was scared. "We need to figure out if there's somewhere outside we can hide."

We were torn between the instructions our moms had given us to stay inside and the fear of what Nick might do. Robert slammed the front door in frustration, causing one of the glass panes to fall out and shatter on the sidewalk.

With the loud noise of the glass breaking, Donna, Diane, and Stacey screamed, thinking Nick had already arrived. Robert paced, trying to decide what to do.

We all debated hiding in the bushes or staying inside with the door locked. We didn't know what to do.

Finally, we decided to stay inside, worried we might get separated if we went outside.

Twenty minutes passed in a tense, fearful silence. My hands felt cold, and my heart pounded in my chest.

Suddenly, we recognized the sound of Nick's car, a brown 1972 Dodge Charger, screeching into the driveway, which was narrow, curved, and flanked by overgrown bushes and a single streetlight nearby casting an eerie glow.

"He's here," Robert whispered, his voice shaking.

The girls were hiding behind the couch but screaming so loud it was making me even more scared.

Nick jumped out of the car, wearing his usual worn-out jean

jacket and jeans and yelling for us to come outside. "Robert! Get out here now! Listen to me! I am your father!"

Like in a movie, somehow, some way, just as Nick was about to enter the apartment, Mom, Vito, and Lori and her boyfriend pulled up in a white 1970 Chevy Impala. Mom jumped out of the car, panic in her eyes. She was yelling at Nick to stay away from us before she was fully out of the car.

Vito ran straight toward the apartment door to confront Nick.

"Stay away from these kids!" Vito yelled, his voice angry.

Nick squared up to Vito, his eyes wild. "You think you can tell me what to do with my family?" he snarled, throwing the first punch.

Vito blocked it and retaliated, hitting Nick weakly on his jaw. "I'm not afraid of you, Nick. You're not taking Donna."

I was surprised Vito knew her name.

Nick lunged at Vito, grabbing him by the collar and dragging him into the house. Robert had opened the door. The two men grappled through the doorway, knocking over a lamp and crashing into the wall. We watched in horror as the fight continued, punches flying and both men grunting in exertion.

"Get in the car!" Lori yelled urgently. Robert and I ran around Nick and Vito, who were now in the living room on the floor. It looked like a wrestling match on TV.

The girls followed our path and ran to Lori, who waved for us to come to her. We all scrambled into the car, crying and screaming.

Nick broke free of Vito and quickly stormed outside. Soon he was holding his lighter to the tailpipe of Lori's car.

"If you start this car and try to take Donna away, I'll blow it up!"

The husband from the apartment next door came out. He was a tall, sturdy man in his forties and wore a white T-shirt and jeans. With Vito, he managed to pull Nick away from the car. The kind woman, his wife, now more visible in her light blue, floral-patterned nightgown, opened her door and guided us into her apartment.

"Come inside, quickly," she said in a calm, soothing voice. "I'll keep you safe."

Her eyes looked nervous as she watched her husband. Once we had all run in, she turned to us.

Inside, she spoke calmly, helping us settle down. We could still hear Nick and Vito yelling in the next apartment, Nick threatening to take Donna and never bring her back.

"We'll protect Donna," Robert whispered to me, both of us determined. I nodded at him, I could see the strength in his eyes.

The woman's husband came back in. "The cops are on their way," he said. "Nick and Vito can't be separated. They're still fighting."

Not long after, the blue and red flashes of a cruiser light reflected on the walls, and we heard the police arrive. Soon, Nick and Vito were handcuffed and taken away. The officers were tall and stern-looking, dressed in their crisp navy-blue uniforms with shiny badges.

"Sorry, ma'am, we're just doing our job," an officer told Mom as she pleaded for Vito. "We'll figure out what happened and release him if that's what needs to happen."

The police officers, calm and authoritative, ensured that everyone was safe before they left.

We watched through the front window, relieved that Nick was going away. The kind blonde lady offered us water or milk. I looked at Robert, relieved but still anxious.

Mom came over to make sure we were all there and okay.

"Thank you so much," Mom said to the kind lady. "Can you stay with the kids for a couple of hours while I handle things at the police station?"

"Of course," the woman replied warmly.

"Thank you," my mom said. "I'm not sure how long it will take."

We stayed with her and her husband, passing the time with some fun activities.

The kind lady brought out a stack of board games like Candy Land and Chutes and Ladders, and we spent the next few hours engrossed in them. Her husband, who introduced himself as Bob, even joined us in a few rounds of Go Fish and War.

After a while, the woman, who we learned was named Alice, made us root beer floats with vanilla ice cream, which we enjoyed on the back porch. We talked about our favorite TV shows, like *The Brady Bunch* and *Scooby-Doo*, and she even let us watch an episode of *Happy Days* on her black-and-white TV.

The night had been so scary, but in the safety of Alice and Bob's home, we found a little peace. They had a collection of comic books, and we all took turns reading issues of *Archie* and *Superman*, laughing at the stories and sharing our favorite parts.

Outside, the summer night was warm and sticky, the air filled with the sounds of crickets and distant traffic.

Wearing our pajamas—me in my Hulk shirt and shorts, Robert in his Bugs Bunny pajamas, and Donna in her pink nightgown—we felt a mix of relief and exhaustion as we settled in for the night, comforted by Alice's gentle words and the safe, cozy environment of her home.

CHAPTER 11

Brain Way Out

3rd Grade

MY MIND WAS WANDERING TODAY MUCH MORE THAN USUAL. I SAT at the kitchen table at home, the late afternoon sun streaming through the window and making long shadows across my math workbook.

It was supposed to be a normal day, just like any other in third grade, but my mind was far from the numbers in front of me. I couldn't stop thinking about Nick, who was more of a monster than a father figure. His anger and violence were like a dark cloud that hung over our house, always threatening to make our days difficult.

The thought of that made me shiver. Even though I was just a kid, I could tell something was seriously wrong with him. He was dangerous, and I hated the way he made us all feel. It was like we were trapped in our own home, walking on eggshells just to keep the peace.

Mrs. Richter, my third-grade teacher, had given us an assignment today to write about how we saw our lives in the future. It was simple, but how could I think about the future when the present was so messed up? After finishing my math, reading, and writing homework, I just sat there, pencil in hand, staring at the blank piece of paper. What did the future even look like for a kid like me?

I started daydreaming, as I often did, about escaping this mess. I knew I wouldn't be a rockstar or a famous athlete. That wasn't me. I wasn't a big guy or good with musical instruments.

I didn't have the outspokenness of my older brother, Robert, who reminded me of J.J. from the TV show *Good Times*. Robert was always cracking jokes, trying to lighten the mood, even when things were at their worst.

I saw myself more like Michael, the younger brother on the show. Michael was smart, and he used his brain to get through tough situations. That's what I wanted to be like. I kept thinking about how Michael always found a way out of trouble, not with his fists, but with his smarts. He didn't let the world around him dictate his future; he carved his own path. That's what I needed to do.

My brain was my ticket out of this mess, I thought. I wasn't going to let Nick's anger define my life. I wanted to be more than just a kid from a broken home, which is what I heard them call it on the news. I wanted to be someone who made a difference, someone who could think their way out of a bad situation.

As I sat there, lost in thought, I imagined a future where Nick was gone from our lives.

We could be a happy family, without fear, without anger. Maybe we'd have a small apartment somewhere. Nothing fancy, but it would be ours. A place where Robert could be his goofball self without worrying about getting hit, where Donna could play without Nick's eyes following her every move, and where Mom could smile and laugh again, the way she used to before Nick came into our lives when I was younger.

In my mind, I saw myself studying hard, getting good grades, and eventually going to college. Maybe I'd become a lawyer or a teacher—something where I could use my brain to help people.

I wasn't sure what I'd do, but I knew I wanted to make a difference. I knew wanted to show people that you could come from a messed-up situation and still make something of yourself.

I thought about Mrs. Richter's assignment again. How did I see my life in the future? I saw a life free from Nick's shadow. A life where I wasn't just surviving but thriving. When I heard people say that about babies and I knew I wanted to be thriving one day. I saw a life where I would use my mind to build a better future for myself and my family. Because if there was one thing I'd learned from watching *Good Times,* it was that even in the toughest situations, there's always hope. You just have to hold on to it and never let go.

I found a pencil and began to write, the words coming more easily than I expected. I wrote about how, even though things were tough right now, I believed that the future could be different. I wrote about how my mom, Robert, Donna, and I could live in a place where we didn't have to be scared all the time. I imagined a small apartment, not too big, but cozy and ours. A place where we could all laugh and be ourselves without fear.

In my assignment, I wrote, "When I grow up, I want to be someone who helps people. Maybe a lawyer or a teacher. I want to go to college and use my brain to make a difference. My brain is my secret superpower, like superheroes have. It's like a magic key that can open doors to new places and possibilities.

"No matter how hard things get, I know that if I keep learning and working hard, I can make a better life for myself and my family. I won't let Nick's anger or anyone else's anger decide my future. I will use my brain to find a way out of this and make a new path for all of us."

I wrote about how I saw myself helping others who might be in tough situations, just like Michael, the brother of J.J. in *Good Times,* used his brain to navigate through problems. I wrote, "I want to show people that even if you come from a messed-up situation, you can still do something great. You can be someone who matters.

"You just have to believe in yourself and never give up. I know that my brain is my ticket out of this mess. It's my way of making sure that one day, we'll all be free from Nick and his anger. One day, we'll have a life that's happy and safe, where we can all be ourselves and not be afraid."

As I finished writing, I looked out the window and saw the sun setting, painting the sky with shades of orange and pink. South Florida sunsets were so beautiful, and for a moment, I let myself get lost in the colors.

Then, the reality of Nick coming home soon snapped me back. The knot of fear in my stomach tightened, but I pushed it down. I had to be strong, not just for me, but for Robert, Donna, and Mom.

As I stared at the last words on my paper, I felt a strange mix of hope and dread.

Nick had disappeared from our lives for a while. The fear of his return was in me, but something else was growing inside me, a sense of determination. That's when my mind began to drift again, this time to the comic books I loved to read. One of my favorite characters wasn't a hero, it was a villain, the Leader from the Hulk comics.

He was a genius, and his name in the comics was Samuel Sterns. He had an extremely large head. He used his enormous intellect for evil, always trying to outsmart the Hulk and everyone else. What if I could be like the Leader, only different? What if I could use my brain for good instead of evil?

I closed my eyes and imagined myself as the Leader. Not the bad one from the comics, a good Leader. In my mind, I had a big, powerful brain that I used to solve problems and help people. I could see it, me standing tall with a green suit and knowledge in my mind. My head was larger than normal, like the Leader's, but instead of using it to hurt others, I used it to create solutions, to think my way out of tough spots, and to protect my family.

In my daydream, I saw myself stepping in front of my mom, Robert, and Donna, holding up my hand to stop Nick in his tracks.

"No more," I said in a confident voice. "You can't hurt us anymore."

Nick tried to get angry, but he couldn't.

I used my super-brain to calm him down, to make him see that his anger was wrong and that he needed to leave us alone. With my big brain, I figured out ways to keep him away, to protect my family from his threats.

It wasn't just about stopping Nick. In my imagination, I used my smarts to help others too. I helped kids who were scared or in trouble, showing them that they could be strong and find their own way out of bad situations. I gave them advice, listened to their stories, and used my big brain to come up with plans that would make their lives better. I was a Leader, different from the one from the comics. I was a leader for good, a protector, a problem-solver.

In this imaginary world, my family was happy. Mom was smiling again, Robert was free to be his fun self, and Donna was safe and carefree. We lived in a sweet, kind home, just like I'd written in my assignment. It was a place full of love and laughter, without the shadow of fear hanging over us. And every time something tough came up, I knew I could handle it. I had the brains to figure things out, to make things right.

If I were the Leader, I would't be just smart, I'd be brave. I'd use my intelligence to stand up for what's right, to protect those who couldn't protect themselves. And most importantly, I used that big brain to carve out a future where we were all free from fear.

I opened my eyes, the image of the good Leader still fresh in my mind. It was just a fantasy, I knew that, but it made me feel stronger. It reminded me that even though I was just a kid, even though I couldn't fight Nick or stop him from being angry, I had something powerful. I had my brain, and that was in my power. I could use it to think of ways to keep my family safe, to plan for a better future, and to hold on to hope.

Looking at the sunset outside, I smiled a little. The colors were fading, the sky turning darker, but I felt a lightness in my heart. Maybe things were tough now, but I believed that they wouldn't always be this way. I had my dreams, my plans, and, well, my brain. And just like the good Leader, I would use them to make things better, to protect the people I loved, and to create a future where we could all be happy and safe.

I picked up my pencil and added a few more lines to my assignment, describing how I imagined myself as the Leader, using my big brain for good. I wrote, "Sometimes, I like to pretend I'm a superhero with a big brain like the Leader from the Hulk comics. Instead of using it for bad things, I use it to help people and make the world a better place. I protect my family and friends, and I find smart ways to solve problems. My brain is my superpower, and I know that with it, I can make a better future for all of us."

As I finished, I felt a sense of satisfaction. It felt real to me. It gave me strength, a vision to hold on to. As I put away my schoolwork, I knew that no matter what happened, I'd keep dreaming and planning. Because in my heart, I believed that one day I could turn those dreams into reality. I could be a good version of the Leader, using my brain to make a difference and to lead my family into a brighter, safer future.

I looked at what I wrote and felt a small spark of hope. It felt possible, like maybe someday it could be true that my brain would keep me safe from Nick.

I knew that as long as I kept using my brain, as long as I kept believing in myself, there was a way out. For now, dreaming and planning were all I had. But I knew that someday, those dreams could become real. I would have to lean on my brain to guide me to a better future.

I took a deep breath and closed my notebook, feeling a little stronger, a little more hopeful. *One day,* I thought, *one day we'll be free from Nick. Free from the monster.*

CHAPTER 12

Car Ride to Court

3rd Grade

I SAT IN THE BACK SEAT OF MOM'S CAR, STARING OUT THE WINDOW as we drove toward the courthouse. It was spring and close to my April birthday, which usually brought a good mood, but my stomach was doing flip-flops, and I felt like I was going to be sick. I wished I could be at home playing video games or watching *Twilight Zone* reruns with my best friend, Keith, instead of heading to talk to a judge about my stepdad.

"Anthony, I know this is hard," Mom said from the driver's seat. She looked at me in the rearview mirror, her eyes full of concern. "But it's really important that you tell the judge what happened."

I nodded, biting my lip. "But what if I mess up, Mom? What if I forget what to say or get something wrong?"

Mom reached back and squeezed my hand. "You won't mess up. Just speak from your heart and tell the truth. Remember, the judge wants to help us. He needs to know what Nick did so he can understand why we need the divorce."

I took a deep breath. "Okay, but what exactly should I say?"

"Just tell him the truth about how Nick treated you and Robert," Mom explained. "Tell him about the times Nick yelled at you, the times he hurt you. It's important that the judge knows everything."

"But what if I say something different than what you told me to say?" I asked, my voice trembling a little. "Will you get in trouble?"

"No, honey," Mom reassured me. "Just tell the truth. That's all that matters. The judge will understand. And don't worry about me, okay? I'll be fine."

How could I not worry? If I lost my mom, if we lost our mom, then we would have no one. *I have to do my best here—better than my best*, I thought. *I have to make sure I don't screw this up.*

"I'll be fine," she said. "And you'll be fine too. No matter what happens."

I nodded again, trying to absorb what she was saying. I knew I had to be brave, but the thought of standing in front of the judge made me feel small and scared. I imagined the judge as this big, intimidating figure, like a principal times ten.

"Will I get arrested if I lie in court?" I asked suddenly, the fear bubbling up inside me.

Mom turned to look at me, her face hardening a bit. "No, Anthony, you won't get arrested. Just be honest. That's all anyone can ask of you. And remember, I'm right here with you. You're not alone."

"What if I say something wrong, though?" I asked, feeling my heart race. "What if the judge thinks I'm lying even if I'm telling the truth?"

Mom sighed gently but firmly. "Anthony, the judge isn't trying to catch you in a lie. He just wants to know what really happened. Just take your time and tell him everything you remember. It'll be okay."

The courthouse looked huge and scary as we pulled into the parking lot. My heart was pounding as we walked inside, our footsteps echoing on the marble floors. Mom held my hand tightly, leading me through the maze of hallways to the courtroom.

"Just remember what we talked about," Mom whispered as we reached the door.

"You can do this, Anthony. I believe in you."

I nodded, swallowing hard. We entered the courtroom, and I immediately noticed the judge sitting at the front. He looked stern but not mean. I took a deep breath, trying to calm down.

The judge called our case, and we walked up to the bench. I felt like my throat was closing up as I stood next to Mom, looking up at the judge, who seemed even taller up close.

"Good morning," the judge said, his voice deep and serious. "I understand we have a young man here who wants to tell me about his experiences. Anthony, is that right?"

I nodded, my voice barely a whisper. "Yes, sir."

"Please, have a seat," the judge said, pointing to a chair. I climbed up into the seat, feeling really small.

"Now, Anthony," the judge began, "I want you to know that this is a safe place.

You can tell me anything, and I will listen. Can you tell me about your stepdad, Nick?"

I glanced at Mom, who gave me an encouraging nod. I took a deep breath and started to speak.

"Nick was . . . really mean to us," I said, my voice shaking. "He would yell at me and my brother Robert all the time. He drank a lot, and he would get really angry.

Sometimes he would hit us."

The judge nodded, looking serious. "That must have been very scary for you."

I nodded, tears starting to fill my eyes. "Yeah, it was. He hurt Robert more because he's older, but he would still hit me too. He didn't hurt Donna because she's his real daughter. He treated us differently I think because we're not his kids, I guess."

"I'm sorry you had to go through that," the judge said gently. "Some stepparents treat their kids wonderfully. Maybe someday you'll find out what that's like."

"Can you tell me about a specific time when Nick hurt you or your brother?"

My mind searched, trying to remember the details. "There was this one time . . . Nick was really mad because Robert didn't do his homework. He grabbed Robert by the arm and pushed him against the wall. Robert was crying. I was so scared. I tried to help, but Nick pushed me away and told me to stay out of it."

The judge listened closely, taking notes. "Thank you for sharing that, Anthony. Is there anything else you want to tell me about Nick?"

I glanced at Mom again, who gave me a look that said I needed to keep going. "Just that . . . we don't want him to come back. Ever. We're scared of him. And we just want to be safe."

"That's very understandable," the judge said. "Can you tell me if Nick ever apologized or tried to make things right after these incidents?"

I shook my head. "No, sir. He never said sorry. He just acted like it was normal to hurt us."

The judge nodded, his face serious. "Thank you for your honesty, Anthony. Your courage today helps me understand what you've been through."

The courtroom stuff was finally over, and I felt a mix of relief and exhaustion as we walked back to the car. Mom hugged me tightly as soon as we were outside.

"You did so well, Anthony," she said, her voice full of pride. "I'm proud of you."

I hugged her back, feeling a little better. "Do you think the judge will help us?"

"I think he will," Mom said with a smile. "You were very brave, and you told the truth. That's all anyone can ask."

As we drove home, I couldn't help but worry about the newspaper ad that my mom had mentioned on the way to seeing the judge. Mom had said we had put an ad in the classified section of the newspaper as a way to notify him of the court date so that he could show up. I was a bit worried he would come to the courthouse, but my mom said she was certain he wouldn't come that day. She was right. He didn't show up.

"Mom, what if Nick sees the newspaper ad? What if he comes back into our life?"

Mom sighed, looking serious. "It's just a few small lines in the classified section of the newspaper, so he's not likely he has seen it or anyone would show it to him. But, it's the law and it's a see risk we had to take. Remember, Anthony, we have a restraining order against him. If he tries to come near us, the police will take care of it. We just have to trust the justice system."

I nodded, still feeling uneasy but reassured by her words. I hoped with all my heart that we would never see Nick again.

Later that day, I met up with my pal Keith at the park. We sat on the swings with the South Florida sun shining down on us as we talked. We loved hanging out at Centennial Park in North Lauderdale, near our grade school, to have our talks. Not many kids went there, so we had the place to ourselves a lot.

"So, how was court?" Keith asked, his eyes wide with curiosity.

"It was scary," I admitted. "I had to talk to the judge about Nick and everything he did to us."

"Wow," Keith said, his voice full of awe. "What did you say?"

"I just told him the truth," I said with a shrug. "I told him how Nick would yell at us and hit us. And how he treated Donna differently because she's his real daughter." "That sounds tough," Keith said sympathetically. "But I knew you could do it."

"Thanks," I said, feeling a little better. "I was really scared I would mess up. I even asked my mom if I would get arrested if I lied in court."

Keith's eyes went wide. "Did she say you would?"

"No," I said with a chuckle that surprised me as it came out. "She said I just had to tell the truth. That's all that matters."

"Did the judge ask you a lot of questions?" Keith asked, while swinging back and forth on the swing.

"Yeah, he did," I said. "He asked me to tell him about a specific time Nick hurt us, and if Nick ever apologized. I told him everything. It was hard, but the judge was patient.

He just wanted to understand what we went through. He asked a lot of questions though."

"Were you nervous?" Keith asked, his eyes full of concern.

"Yeah, I was super nervous," I admitted. "I was afraid I'd mess up or say something wrong. But Mom kept telling me to just tell the truth, and that's what I did."

"Do you think the judge will help you guys?" Keith asked.

"I hope so," I said, my voice trembling a little. "Mom says he will, but I'm still scared. What if Nick sees the newspaper ad about the hearing? What if he comes back?"

Keith looked worried. "Do you think he would?"

"I don't know," I said, kicking at the ground with my hands in my pockets. "But we have a restraining order. The police will help if he tries to come near us, my mom says. I just hope we never have to see him again."

Keith nodded thoughtfully. "Well, I'm glad you told the truth. And I hope the judge helps you guys out.»

"Me too," I said, looking up at the sky. "But I'm worried Nick will try to take Donna. She's his real daughter, and he always said he wants her back."

Keith's eyes widened. "That would be terrible. Do you think he could do that?"

"I don't know," I admitted, feeling a knot in my stomach. "But Mom says we have to trust the system. I just hope the judge makes sure we're safe."

Keith leaned closer. "Why are you worried about seeing Nick again, Anthony?

What do you think will happen if he comes back?"

I sighed, feeling the tension in my chest. "I'm scared that if Nick comes back, he'll try to hurt us again. Or even worse, he might try to take Donna away from us. I don't know what he'd do, but I just know it won't be good."

Keith looked serious. "That sounds really scary. But you have your mom and the police to protect you. And I'm here for you too."

"Thanks, Keith," I said, feeling a bit of relief. "I'm glad you're here for me. It helps to know you kinda understand. Well, as much as you can. I know it's not easy to hear all of this, so thanks."

"I don't get all of it," Keith said. "I just know it sounds pretty awful. I don't know how all of you have put up with it for so long."

We stopped swinging but kept talking, sitting on the swings, feet touching the ground.

I felt a mix of relief and some nervousness. I had faced my fears and told the truth, but the uncertainty about the future still gnawed at me. With Mom helping and my best pal supporting me, I felt like I could handle almost anything.

Nevertheless, I couldn't shake the worry that we hadn't seen the last of Nick. I was relieved the day was over, but I was uncertain about what lay ahead.

I thought, *What if he comes back? Can I live my life like this? Mom says we can't afford to move to a different house.*

I knew I had to be smart in order to get out of this situation. Just like J.J.'s brother, Michael, on *Good Times*.

I'll be like him, I thought.

I looked at the sun and started thinking about how much I feared the monster in the front seat. I didn't ever want to sit behind him again.

CHAPTER 13

The Monster Returns

3rd Grade

MY HEART POUNDED AS I WALKED TO THE BACK OF THE CLASSROOM. It was fall, and I was clutching my Hulk figurine in my hand. I loved the angry look on his face and how when I squeezed his head it would give him a funny look, which made me laugh on the inside. Hulk's purple pants had circular rips just at the knees.

As I walked, I thought to myself how good this Hulk looked. He looked just like the Hulk in the comics.

I distracted myself with the Hulk toy. I found myself squeezing him when things would get stressful. I leaned on him for support.

It made me forget my worries. Sometimes I would daydream about the latest comic book issue or wonder what was going to happen in the next one. I loved the Hulk.

Mrs. Richter had just given us some time to work on our assignments, but I needed to talk to her. I glanced at the green felt poster with Snoopy dressed as an astronaut hanging on the wall. "The Moon is Made of American Cheese," it read. It always made me smile. I could use a smile right now.

"Mrs. Richter," I whispered, trying not to interrupt the quiet of the classroom. She looked up from her desk, her eyes softening when she saw me. She had that look again, the one she always gave me when she knew something was wrong. "Anthony, come sit down," she said, patting the chair next to her. Mrs. Richter might have seemed strict and grumpy to some of the kids, but to me, she was like a second mom. Especially this year, in third grade, she had been supportive so many times.

I took a deep breath and sat down. "Mrs. Richter, I need to talk to you about something," I said, my voice barely above a whisper. I fiddled with the Hulk's tiny green arms, trying to find the right words.

She nodded, her grumpy demeanor melting away into one of concern. "What is it, Anthony? You know you can tell me anything."

I looked down at the Hulk, then back up at her. "It's about Nick, my dad."

Her eyes widened just a little, but she didn't say anything. She just waited for me to continue, which made me feel like I could really talk to her.

"I'm scared he's going to come back," I said, my voice trembling. "He used to hurt me and my brother Robert. He didn't hurt our sister Donna, but hurt us. And I'm scared he's going to come back and hurt us again. Or maybe even take Donna away."

Mrs. Richter reached out and put a hand on my shoulder. "Anthony, I'm so sorry. It's not fair that you have to worry about something like this."

I felt a tear start to slide down my cheek. I quickly wiped it away.

"I just don't know what to do. I don't want him to come back. I don't want to get hurt again."

She squeezed my shoulder gently. "Have you talked to your mom about this? Does she know how scared you are?"

I nodded. "Yeah, she knows. She helped me a lot when we had to go to court. But I'm still scared."

Mrs. Richter nodded sweetly. "It's okay to be scared, Anthony. But I want you to remember something. You're a strong kid. I've seen you grow so much this year. You have more confidence now, and you're doing so well in school. You remind me a lot of my own son when he was your age."

I smiled a little. Mrs. Richter had shown me some of her son's stuff from when he was a little kid, like the Snoopy poster and a collection of *Peanuts* books that I loved to read. She even brought me Bicentennial 1976 quarters sometimes because she knew I liked to collect them.

"I believe in you, Anthony," she continued. "And I know your mom is doing everything she can to keep you and your brother and sister safe. But if you ever feel scared or need someone to talk to, you can always come to me. Okay?"

I nodded again, feeling a little better. "Thanks, Mrs. Richter."

She smiled and handed me a *Peanuts* paperback book from her desk. "Why don't you take a little break and read this? I know how much you love Charlie Brown and Snoopy."

I smiled and took the yellow and red book. It had Charlie Brown on the cover in his baseball uniform on the pitcher's mound.

"Thanks, Mrs. Richter. You're the best."

As I walked back to my seat, I felt a little lighter. Mrs. Richter knew what to say to make me feel better. I opened the book and started reading about Charlie Brown and his friends, letting the comic strips take me away from my worries for a while. I knew I still had a lot to deal with, but with Mrs. Richter on my side, I felt like I could handle anything.

The feeling of relief didn't last long. As the days went by, for whatever reason, the fear of Nick coming back grew stronger. It was like instinct or intuition. One day, after we had finished our math test, Mrs. Richter noticed me staring blankly at my desk, my hands shaking slightly. She walked over and knelt beside me.

"Anthony, why don't you come to the back of the room with me for a bit?" she suggested gently.

I nodded and followed her, feeling my stomach churn with anxiety. We sat down in our usual spot, away from the other kids.

"Tell me what's been bothering you," she said softly, her eyes full of concern.

"I can't stop thinking about Nick," I confessed, my voice a whisper. "Every time I hear a noise outside, I'm scared it's him coming back. What if he hurts me and Robert again? Or worse, what if he takes Donna away?"

Mrs. Richter's face grew even more serious. She took a deep breath and leaned in closer. "Anthony, I understand how terrifying this must be for you. You've been through so much, and it's not fair that you have to deal with these fears."

Tears welled up in my eyes. "I just want to feel safe, Mrs. Richter. I don't want to be scared all the time."

She reached out and held my hand. "You are allowed to feel safe, Anthony. And you deserve to be happy and carefree, just like any other kid. Have you and your mom thought about talking to someone who can help, like a counselor?"

I shook my head. "I don't know. Mom's been really busy trying to keep everything together. She works so hard, and I don't want to make things harder for her. I don't think we have time for that."

Mrs. Richter sighed. She looked worried. "I know your mom is doing her best and she loves you very much, but sometimes it's okay to ask for extra help. There are people out there who can support you and your family through this."

I squinted, feeling both fear and hope. "Do you really think things can get better?"

She nodded firmly. "Yes, I do. I've seen how strong you are, Anthony. You've faced so much already, and you're still here, doing your best every day. That takes a lot of courage. And you have a lot of people who care about you, including me."

I felt a warm feeling spread through my chest. "Thank you, Mrs. Richter. I don't know what I'd do without you."

She smiled, her eyes shining with kindness. "You're never alone, Anthony. Remember that. And whenever you need to talk or just need a break, you can always come to me."

I nodded, feeling a little more hopeful. As I walked back to my desk, I clutched my Hulk figurine a little tighter. *Maybe things will get better*, I thought. *Maybe, with people like Mrs. Richter in my life, I could find a way to feel safe again.*

A few days later, after school, I stayed behind to help Mrs. Richter clean up the classroom. It was something I enjoyed doing, and it gave me a chance to talk to her without other kids around.

"Anthony, I brought something for you," Mrs. Richter said, reaching into her bag.

She pulled out a small, worn notebook. "This was my son's journal when he was about your age. He used to write down his thoughts and feelings, especially when he was going through tough times. This one is blank. He filled other journals. I spoke with him and he wanted you to have it. I thought you might find it helpful to write your thoughts in here."

I took the notebook, feeling the weight of it in my hands. "Thank you, Mrs. Richter. I'll take good care of it."

She smiled warmly. "I know you will. And remember, writing down your feelings can sometimes help you understand them better. It's a way to let them out instead of keeping them all inside."

I nodded, feeling grateful for her constant support. "I'll give it a try."

As I walked home that day, the notebook tucked safely in my backpack, I felt a little spark of hope. Maybe writing down my fears could help me deal with them. And with Mrs. Richter's support, I knew I wasn't alone.

A week later, I sat at the back of the classroom during free time, my notebook open in front of me. I had started writing about my worries, about Nick, and about my hopes for the future.

It felt good to get the words out, even if they were just on paper.

Mrs. Richter walked by and gave me an encouraging smile. "How's the journal going, Anthony?"

I smiled back. "It's helping, I think. Thank you for giving it to me."

I knew this feeling was of pure joy. I wondered how long it had been since I last felt it.

She nodded. "I'm glad to hear that. Remember, you're stronger than you think, and you have a lot of people who care about you."

I thought about how unusual it was to hear these words. They felt like a warm blanket. *I like this feeling,* I thought.

I felt a surge of warmth and gratitude. "I know. And I'm really grateful for that."

As I continued writing, I felt a little more hopeful about the future. I'd still have moments of fear and doubt, but with Mrs. Richter's support, and my mom and brother, I felt a little more ready to face whatever was going to come my way. I started to feel hopeful.

The school bell rang, signaling the end of the day. I packed up my things, carefully tucking the notebook Mrs. Richter had given me into my backpack. As I walked out of the classroom, I felt a sense of calm. Mrs. Richter's words always stayed with me, giving me strength.

When I reached the school gate, I saw my mom standing there. That was unusual.

She almost never picked me up from school.

"Mom?" I called out, hurrying over to her.

She looked tense, her eyes scanning the area around us. "Anthony, we need to leave quickly. I need you to find your brother Robert and meet me back at the car with Donna. Hurry, sweetheart."

My heart sank. "Mom, what's going on?"

She leaned down, her voice urgent but soft. "Nick is back in town. He's looking for Donna. We need to get home and grab a few things before he finds us. Maybe we shouldn't go home. I don't know. I just don't know."

I felt fear in my gut.

I nodded quickly to my mom. "I'll find Robert. We'll be in the car in a minute."

I knew I had to reach inside me and find superpower when things got rough, especially for my mom;

I would get tough. *It's what she needs me to be*, I would think. *Get tough!*

I ran through the schoolyard, my eyes searching for Robert. I found him near the basketball court, talking to his friends.

"Robert!" I yelled, running up to him. "We have to go. If we leave now, we can escape him!"

Within minutes, my bother and I, my mom and sister were in the car. Mom already had Donna in the car with her. We drove off toward the house of my mom's new friend. Nick didn't know this friend, so we knew we'd be safe there.

We never knew if Nick was in town that day or not.

CHAPTER 14

Feeling Protective

4th Grade

"WELCOME TO FOURTH GRADE! I'M YOUR TEACHER, MISS SHELTON, and it's my first year teaching. I'm so excited to teach all of you," Miss Shelton said, her voice brimming with energy and enthusiasm.

As I looked at Miss Shelton, I couldn't help but think about how pretty she was. Like my mom, except her hair was dark. She was the first woman besides my mom who I'd noticed was so pretty. She had this way of speaking that captured everyone's attention in the class. I had heard the word "captivated" on a TV show once, and now I thought I knew what it meant. I was feeling that right now.

She was in a dress, something I had not noticed before on a woman, at least not like this. I liked it. My mind wandered, wondering if I'd seen anyone else in a dress in real life before. Miss Shelton's dress was colorful and flowed as she moved. It added to her personality.

She gave us details about her plans for the year. As she talked, I thought, *Yippee! I finally feel a little happier at home. I'm excited to have a young teacher with so much energy this year.*

I didn't know teachers could be this young, I thought to myself.

She told us she had just graduated from college. That seemed so grown-up and cool to me.

I glanced over at my new friend, Jason, who sat a few rows ahead of me. He caught my eye and gave me a thumbs-up. We'd been friends since the first day of the school year, and we told each other everything. I knew he thought Miss Shelton was pretty too because he had said so during lunch yesterday.

As I started my first assignment with my deskmate, Diana, I felt a high level of enthusiasm and energy. I sat up straight, hoping Miss Shelton would notice me. I liked her voice. It was soft but strong, and she easily held the attention of the entire class. Her excitement about teaching excited me about today's work.

I pulled out my notebook and started writing about our goals for the year, just as she had asked us to. My handwriting was a little messy, but I was trying my best. Every now and then, I glanced up at her, hoping to catch her eye. I felt a flutter in my chest every time she smiled or looked my way.

Miss Shelton walked around the classroom, checking on everyone's progress.

When she got to my desk, she leaned in to see my work.

"Great job, Anthony! Keep it up," she said with a smile that made my heart race.

"Thank you, Miss Shelton," I managed to say, my voice barely above a whisper. Her praise made me feel proud and even more determined to do well. I wanted to impress her, to show her that I was a good student.

During recess, I watched her as she talked with some of the other teachers. She was laughing and seemed so happy. I told myself that one day I would make her laugh like that too. I wanted her to think of me as her favorite student.

Jason came over and nudged me. "She's really nice, isn't she?" he said, looking over at Miss Shelton.

"Yeah, she is," I replied, feeling a bit shy about admitting how much I liked her. "Do you think she likes basketball?" Jason asked, looking thoughtful.

"I don't know, but maybe we can ask her," I suggested, feeling a bit bolder with Jason next to me.

As the days went by, my crush on Miss Shelton only grew stronger. I found myself daydreaming about her, imagining that she was proud of me and that I was her favorite. I worked hard on my assignments and tried to be helpful in class, hoping she would notice my efforts.

One day, during a math lesson, Miss Shelton posed a challenging question to the class. Hands shot up all around me, but I knew the answer. I raised my hand confidently.

"Yes, Anthony?" she called on me.

"The answer is 42. It's because when you multiply 7 and 6, you get 42," I explained, feeling a rush of excitement.

"Exactly right, Anthony! Great job!" she exclaimed, her face lighting up with pride. "Class, did you notice how Anthony explained his answer? That's the kind of thinking we want to see!"

I beamed with pride, feeling like I was on top of the world. I wasn't used to this level of enthusiasm from a teacher. She was a like a big kid, I thought. Moments like these made me feel closer to Miss Shelton.

One day, Miss Shelton announced that we would be doing a special project where we would have to write about someone who inspired us. Without hesitation, I decided to write about her. I poured my heart into the assignment, describing how her enthusiasm and kindness made me excited to learn.

When it was time to hand in our projects, I felt a mix of nerves and excitement. I hoped she liked what I'd written.

A few days later, she returned our assignments, and I saw a big smile drawn on mine. She'd written a note at the bottom: "Anthony, this is a wonderful piece. I'm so proud of you!"

Her words made me feel like I was walking on air.

From that day on, I was even more determined to do my best

in school. Miss Shelton had become my inspiration, and I looked forward to each day in her class, eager to learn and make her proud.

Whenever I finished my schoolwork super early, Miss Shelton noticed. She started letting me read books in the back of the class when I was done. I loved reading, especially adventure stories. My stack of books kept getting taller every week, and I got to explore new adventures and stories almost every day.

One day, after class, Miss Shelton asked me to stay behind. I felt a pang of nervousness and a glimmer of excitement.

"Anthony, can I talk to you for a moment?" she asked kindly.

"Sure, Miss Shelton," I said, my voice a little shaky.

"I've noticed how hard you've been working and how much you love reading," she said. "You're doing such an amazing job, and I want you to know that I see it."

"Thank you, Miss Shelton," I said, my heart swelling with pride.

"I was thinking," she said, "if you'd like, we could start a little book club. Just you and me. We can pick a book to read together and discuss it. What do you think?"

I couldn't believe my ears. "Really? That sounds awesome!"

"Great! We'll start next week. I'll bring the first book, and we'll go from there," she said, her eyes bright with excitement. I had already begun to wonder which book she would pick.

I couldn't stop thinking about her or which book she would pick as I walked home from school with my brother Rob that day. I watched all the cars as they drove by as we made our way to 7-Eleven to get Slurpees.

I wondered what kind of car she drove, if I would see her, and if she would see me walking with my brother. I looked at all the cars as they passed, wondering if I would spot her or even if she went this way to go home.

When we went into 7-Eleven, I became distracted and thought about whether I wanted a Coke or cherry Slurpee.

A couple of months later, Miss Shelton started talking to me a lot more when I finished my work before others in my class. One day, after class, she took me outside and asked me all kinds of questions about my life. I told her about some of the tough times at home and more about happy moments. She listened like she really cared.

Later, we were excitedly reading the book that she picked, *The Dark is Rising,* by Susan Cooper, which was one that was in the back of her room. I told her, with excitement, my thoughts on the book, and then she stopped reading, semi-closed the book, and looked at me.

"Anthony, how would you like to go to Ocean World with me? It's in Fort Lauderdale, not too far from here."

My eyes grew wide...

"Really, Miss Shelton? Ocean World? I've always wanted to go there!"

"Yes, really," she said with a big smile. "We'll see all the sea creatures, watch the shows, and have a great time."

"I think they have a big whale there too," I said. I couldn't believe that she wanted to take me to Ocean World, or take me anywhere, actually. And on a non-school day. I would get to see her on an extra day that I wouldn't usually see her. I was so happy!

After that, Miss Shelton talked about our Ocean World trip all the time. I couldn't wait! Every week, I got more and more excited. She promised it was going to happen soon, and I believed her and looked forward to it. I counted down the days and dreamed about all the amazing things we would see and do at Ocean World. It was going to be the best day ever!

The next day was field day outside on the school grounds in

the morning. The sun was hot and heated up the blacktop, making the whole area bright.

Soon we were in the middle of a fun basketball game, and I dribbled the ball, loving the feeling of the different texture of a basketball under my fingers. I had played basketball before but never in a game like this. I saw Jason waving at me, trying to show he was open.

"Over here, Anthony!" he shouted, full of excitement.

I passed the ball to him and watched as he tried to dodge past our classmates to make a shot. The ball bounced off the rim and started rolling toward the sidelines where Miss Shelton was standing and cheering for us.

She always cheered us on. Today was no different.

I saw the ball rolling toward her and instinctively moved to go after it, but she was already backing up to get it herself. She didn't see the edge of the court and suddenly stumbled onto the grass.

I watch her try to get her balance. My heart skipped a beat. I could see, she was going to fall.

Miss Shelton twisted just enough so she would land on her hands, and I felt relief. Then I noticed she was about to land backward and her skirt was about to fly up over her head.

As fast as I could, I ran over and pushed her skirt down. I heard giggles from some kids, but I didn't care. I tried to make sure Miss Shelton wasn't embarrassed by her skirt going up.

She looked up at me, her cheeks red, and quickly got to her feet and brushed herself off.

"I'm all right, everyone," she called out, her voice steady and calm. The game resumed, and everyone seemed to forget the whole thing quickly. Soon, the school bell rang, signaling the end of recess.

As we walked back toward the school building, Miss Shelton caught up to me. She leaned down and whispered, "Thank you for looking out for me, Anthony. That was very kind of you."

I felt a swell of pride in my chest and said, "You're welcome, Miss Shelton," as my face warmed.

Just outside the building, I noticed a bunch of kids near the playground, crowded around our classmate, Lucy. I ran over to see what was happening. Lucy had a small bird perched on her finger. It was the brightest blue I'd ever seen. The bird was relaxed, hopping from finger to finger as Lucy giggled.

Miss Shelton had followed me and smiled when she saw the bird. "Looks like you've made a new friend, Lucy," she said with warmth in her voice.

Lucy beamed. "We're explorers, Miss Shelton! This bird is our guide."

We all watched as the bird spread its wings and flew off into the sky. We stood there, staring up until it disappeared. The bell rang again, and we headed back inside.

Back in the classroom, Miss Shelton started our next lesson. I looked around at my classmates, glad to be part of such a good group. I looked up at Miss Shelton, who saw me and smiled.

As the lesson went on, my mind drifted back to the playground. I was lucky to be part of moments like this. Life was starting to feel different.

I felt different inside as I looked around at the class. *I like his feeling*, I thought.

The sun shone outside, and inside the classroom, it felt just as bright.

As I noticed the brightness, I realized I felt bright like the sun too. It made me nervous to feel this happy. I couldn't help but think something terrible was right around the corner.

CHAPTER 15

The Long Walk Home

4th Grade

THE MID-AFTERNOON SUN MADE LONG SHADOWS FROM THE PALM trees and grass in the lawns in North Lauderdale, Florida. I looked at Robert as we walked home from school.

His middle school wasn't close by, but today, for some reason, he met me at my school, North Lauderdale Elementary, which is where he had gone to school too. I was in fourth grade, our sister Donna was in first grade at the same school as me, and Robert now attended Margate Middle School for sixth grade.

"Hi Ant," Robert said.

"Hi Rob," I said.

We walked in silence for a few minutes.

My gut told me not to ask him why he was here today. *If it's bad news,* I thought, *I don't want to know right away. If it's good news, he'll tell me when he wants to tell me.* "Hope for good news, expect bad," my mom always said.

"Hey, Ant," Robert said. "Remember how bad things were with Nick?"

I nodded, kicking a pebble along the sidewalk. "Yeah, it was really tough. I can't believe Mom finally left him."

"She had to after what he did. Burning holes in the couch, yelling all the time, and hitting us and well . . . I didn't think we'd ever be able to escape him."

"I knew Mom would eventually figure out a way to escape," I said. "I feel like she stopped loving him a while ago. I could feel it coming. Could you?"

"Yes," Robert said. "I'm so glad she did. I wasn't sure if he would ever let us leave."

"She tried really hard to keep us together and tried so hard to make it work as a family," I said. "Especially because we moved here from New York when we were little, leaving behind our aunts and uncles and cousins, to start a new life. Mom had to make it work here."

We walked quietly for about a few minutes.

"Things feel better now," I said.

Robert looked at me. His face turned serious.

"You know why I came to your school today, right?"

I shook my head. "Nope, why?"

"Mom heard through some friends that Nick might be back in town. She came by school during her lunch break and got me permission to leave early so I could come here. She didn't want us walking alone."

My heart skipped a beat. "You think he'll try to find us?"

"Maybe," Rob said. "I think he will, actually. It's not like we live in a different house. He knows where we live. It's just in between home and school that I'm worried about. We have to be extra careful with Donna. We know he wants to take her."

As we neared the corner where we usually met Donna, I saw she wasn't there. My stomach tightened with worry.

"Where is she?" I asked, looking all around us.

Robert's face turned fearful. "She knows how dangerous it is. What if . . . What if Nick took her?"

"Maybe she went home with friends," I said. "She's probably fine."

Robert's eyes filled with tears. "I can't believe it. He took her this time. He really did it."

"We need to hurry," I said. "Maybe she's on her way home."

Robert walked faster, his steps almost a jog. I struggled to keep up with him, my heart pounding in my chest.

The green grass and palm trees that typically made our walk home feel pleasant felt blurry as we sped toward home.

"Anthony, what if he really took her?" Robert's voice cracked.

"We'll find her," I said, trying to sound braver than I felt. "She's smart. She knows to stay away from him."

"What if she didn't have a choice?" Robert's eyes were full of tears.

I felt tears forming in my own eyes. *No time to cry,* I thought.

"We have to get home," I said, my voice barely above a whisper. "Maybe she's there."

We started running, our sneakers loud against the sidewalk. Every step felt long, even as we ran. My mind raced with terrible thoughts about Nick. Kidnapping felt different. This was a new feeling. Dread.

Could he really do that? I wondered.

"Anthony, I really think he took her. I really, really think he took her," Robert said, his voice shaking as we ran.

"I'm secretly hoping that he didn't," I said. "I'm worried too. It feels like he took her."

We were jogging now, feeling tired as our hearts raced. The mile felt so long.

Time felt too slow. We started running faster again.

I had a feeling of doom. I ran faster. If something bad had happened or there was danger, I wanted to know right away.

As we turned onto our street, Southwest Eighth Street, my heart leaped.

There, in the driveway of the second house from the corner, was Donna with her friend Kenny. Relief washed over me immediately. I felt like I could collapse from the weight of the feeling.

"Donna!" Robert called out, his voice shaky.

Robert and I looked at each other in disbelief. We were shocked she was really there.

"We were so worried!" Robert exclaimed.

I was surprised he was able to speak at that moment.

Donna looked up, confused. "I got a ride home with Kenny's mom and dad. We got here right after school. We've been playing."

I knelt down to her level and calmly said, "Donna, you can't do that again. You have to wait for us or me at school, no matter what. Promise?"

Donna saw the look in my eyes and nodded. "I promise. I'm sorry, Ant. I didn't think it was a bad idea."

"It's okay, just stay with us next time," Robert said, still shaken.

I could tell that Robert was full of fear and anger. I was scared too. We knew yelling at her would just upset her. We stopped ourselves from sharing how scared we really were so that she wouldn't be walking around full of fear all the time.

"Let's go inside," Robert said.

He led the way.

Donna and Kenny followed us into the house. We told them to stay inside and play. We asked Kenny's mom if they could play inside because it was too hot outside.

"I didn't want to make her nervous," Robert told me. "Mom says not to tell the neighbors or Kenny's parents about what might happen. It's just better if they stay inside.

Then Nick can't see them if he drives down the block."

We stepped outside of Kenny's house and stared at each other. We quickly scanned the block for Nick's car.

We then stared at each other, speechless. We again checked the street in both directions, paused, and then turned right to go down the block toward our house.

We talked and walked past the ten houses from Kenny's house to our house. As we walked, I gave Robert an update about my lawn mowing service. Robert had helped me when I started mowing lawns in the neighborhood, but he didn't like it. So, my best friend, Chuck, who lived next door to Kenny, became my lawn mowing partner.

"You see this house here?" I pointed to a neatly trimmed lawn. "That's one of my regulars now. A new customer. A&C Lawn Service at your service."

Robert raised an eyebrow. "A&C Lawn Service?"

"Yeah, you know, Anthony and Chuck's Lawn Service. I just got T-shirts made with 'A&C Lawn Service' on the back," I said proudly. "And guess what? I put this iron-on patch on the front of Ayatollah Khomeini with a screw. Our customers love it."

Robert laughed. "That's funny. Where'd you get the T-shirts?"

"Right next to Kmart on 441, in that set of stores, is a T-shirt shop just like the ones in the strip of stores on Pompano Beach," I told him. "The shirts were five dollars each if I bought two. Got one for me and one for Chuck."

"That's cool," Robert said.

"I'll get you one too, if you want," I said. "If I have to get two again, I'll get one for Donna too."

"No thanks," Robert said.

"I bought two new lawn mowers from Kmart. Got 'em for $99 each, on sale."

"Sounds like you guys are really getting into mowing more lawns," Robert said.

"We are. We have about five regular customers now, and we'll get more," I said, feeling a surge of pride. "I want to get everyone on the block to be a customer."

"Do you ever get tired of mowing lawns?" Robert asked.

"Nope. I love the feeling of when the lawn is done," I said. "I know most of our neighbors from knocking on their doors, collecting their newspapers to recycle."

"You still doing that?" Robert asked.

"Uncle Bernie takes me once a month to get money for the newspapers at the place where they weigh your car on the way in, you dump your paper, and then they pay you on the way out after they weigh the car again," I said. "It's in the bad part of Pompano Beach, but it's so cool. You should come with us sometime. It's like a big industrial junkyard!"

"Nah," Robert said. "Maybe spend less time on the newspapers and more time on the lawns. You'll make more money. And you can expand the business when you're older."

"Yeah, that's the idea," I said. "We want to get more customers and maybe even hire a couple of other kids to help out. I think Doug would be good. Then maybe Leo, who lives close. We could be the biggest lawn service in North Lauderdale!"

"That would be cool, Ant," Robert said, smiling.

"I hate mowing laws, otherwise I'd help out," he said. "I don't have the patience for it. It's a pain."

"I get it, Rob," I said. "You have to love it to do it."

We walked past another house with a newly mowed lawn.

"This guy tips us if we weed his garden after mowing and trimming."

"That's cool," Robert said. "You can buy all the candy you want."

"Yeah, I like 3 Musketeers the most," I said. "And I like not having to bug Mom for money."

We were silent for a few minutes.

"I like when it's quiet," I said. "Feels so different than our walk home from school."

"Right?" Rob said. "Oh, man. I really thought he had taken her!"

"I did too, Rob," I said. "We really got lucky today. Maybe luck is finally on our side. My teacher says if you think you're lucky, you will be."

"Maybe I'll try that," Robert said. "All I know is I'm starving. It's good to be home!"

"Uh, we've got a problem, Rob," I called out, looking in the fridge. "There's not much here."

"What's there?" he asked.

"Just a half-empty jar of Peter Pan peanut butter and some jelly," I said.

"How about saltines?" Rob said, bringing over the blue and white box. "We could make peanut butter and jelly crackers with those."

"Desperate times call for desperate measures, I guess," I said with a laugh. "I'm not really feeling the PB and J vibe though."

"I'll have these," I said, a bag of frozen hot dog buns in my hands. "I'll toast them and put some butter on them."

After a few minutes, Robert took a bite of his PB and J cracker and said, "This isn't too bad."

"These are actually pretty good too," I said, taking a big bite of one of the buttered hot dog buns. "I love to bite into the crispy edges. Crisis averted!"

"Mom's making Hamburger Helper tonight," I said. "The spaghetti and meatball one."

"That's my favorite," Robert said with a smile.

"Let's watch channel 45," I said. "*Leave It to Beaver* and *Father Knows Best* come on next. Let's watch and do our chores after that. They'll still get done before Mom gets home from work."

An hour later, we wrapped up our chores.

"Okay, bro, let's go get Donna," Rob said.

"Let's run to Kenny's house," I said as we went outside.

"Donna, you really scared us today," Robert said as we left

Kenny's house with her. "We really thought something bad happened."

"I'm really sorry, Rob," Donna said, looking up at him with her big blue eyes, from behind her long brown curly hair. "I won't do it again."

"It's okay, Donna," I said, squeezing her hand as we walked home. "We're just glad you're okay."

Soon, Mom was home from work.

"Thank you for looking out for Donna," she said, hugging us when she came in the front door. "I'm sorry you had to worry so much."

"It's okay, Mom," Robert said. "We just wanted to keep her safe."

"We'll always protect her," I said.

Mom sat down, looking tired.

"You know, you boys are amazing," she said softly. "I know this is all difficult stuff, and you're just kids, but you've stepped up and been responsible way beyond your years. I'm really thankful for that."

"We just want to help, Mom," Robert said.

"I know you do," she said. "Thank you. Just thank you. Thank you both. It's not easy for me to be at work with all of this uncertainty lurking around us, but knowing I have you two looking out for each other and for Donna helps make it doable."

We all hugged.

"You boys are my men. I don't know what I'd do without you."

"We're here for you, Mom," I said with a lump in my throat.

Robert said, "We're in this together, Mom!"

Mom made us one of her usual dinners. She had a few go-to dinners that she could make fast: Hamburger Helper, noodles and cottage cheese, or pasta and sauce.

Tonight was Hamburger Helper night.

"The Hamburger Helper tasted better than ever," I said. "So good with the ground beef."

"We have each other, and that gives me so much comfort," Mom said. "We are a family, and we will keep fighting hard, protecting each other. I'll make a special surprise dessert tonight!"

CHAPTER 16

Ocean World Saturday

4th Grade

It was a Saturday morning, and the sun was bright in the sky. I felt like my heart was about to burst out of my chest. The excitement was too much. I was practically bouncing as I got ready. Today was the day Miss Shelton would be taking me to Ocean World. I couldn't believe it!

Our house in South Florida was a typical 1974 ranch style: one floor, with ugly red carpet and ugly silver and black wallpaper. Nick, who hung wallpaper and painted houses, used to bring home the ugliest leftover paint and wallpaper from his job, Mom would say and complain to Nick about it before he left us.

"I can't stand these paint colors and the unattractive wallpaper," Mom said, shaking her head as she stirred Italian sauce on the stove. "At least we have something on the walls. I guess I can't complain too much."

I had already changed my shirt three times, trying to decide between my Tasmanian Devil and Yosemite Sam T-shirts. My mom noticed my T-shirt dilemma.

"How many times are you gonna change your shirts, Anthony? Just pick one and be done with it," she told me, exasperated.

"I just wanna make sure I look good for Miss Shelton and wear the right shirt," I replied, trying to hide my nervousness. "I don't know which cartoon character she likes better. I think it's Yosemite Sam. Maybe it's the Tasmanian Devil. I'm honestly not sure."

"Hey, Mom, can you help me pick out a shirt? Which one do you think she would like better?" I asked.

"I have no idea," she said, shaking her head.

I decided on the Yosemite Sam T-shirt because it matched well with my shorts. I put on my Kmart Trax sneakers and pulled up my white socks with aqua and orange stripes like the colors the Miami Dolphins NFL football team wore. My entire outfit, from head to toe, was from Kmart. Mom had worked there recently, and we shopped there all the time. The clothes were sturdy and cheap, Mom would say, perfect for a nine-year-old boy.

I made myself toast with peanut butter and jelly, my go-to breakfast, while Mom made lunch for Robert and Donna.

Robert and Donna told me they wished they were going too, and Donna said she was happy for me. They knew how much I was looking forward to this trip and how much I liked Miss Shelton.

"You're so lucky, Anthony," Robert said, munching on his cereal. "I wish I could go to Ocean World with you, but I'm hanging out with my friends."

"Yeah, have fun!" Donna said, her eyes big. I could see she was excited for me.

"Tell us all about it when you get back! Me and mom are going shopping today."

For months, Miss Shelton had been telling me about this Saturday. She had to delay the trip a few times from February to April because of personal reasons. I didn't mind at all. The delays meant there were more conversations about Ocean World throughout the school year, and I secretly hoped we'd keep talking about it until the summer.

I liked talking with Miss Shelton. She was thoughtful. She had told me in one of our first conversations in the back of the classroom when I was done with my schoolwork that this was her first job out of college. She seemed to really like me, and we would chat a lot about school or home or life or whatever. Sometimes, I imagined she wanted to adopt me. I knew it was a total daydream, but it made me feel special.

She had told me that this trip was partly to celebrate my birthday and to thank me for being such a sweet kid all year. I didn't care why we were doing it; I was just glad we were going.

When she was about to arrive, I stood by the window and looked for her maroon Chevrolet Nova. I knew the car well because every day after school, I would walk slowly—slowing down me and my brother, who would get annoyed at me—just so I could watch Miss Shelton drive by and maybe wave.

Just as I had imagined her car driving by on a walk home from school with my brother, her car pulled into our driveway.

I yelled, "Mom! I'll see you later! I'll be home before dinner!"

I sprinted out the door. I felt like the luckiest kid in the world. The maroon Chevy car door was heavy as I opened it and climbed into the front seat. Miss Shelton looked different today. She was dressed casually and pretty, wearing blue jeans and a striped blouse, unlike the dresses she wore to school.

"Hi, Anthony! Are you ready for our big day at Ocean World?" she asked, her smile bright.

"Yes, Miss Shelton! Thank you so much for taking me," I said, trying to keep my voice steady. I couldn't hide my excitement. "This is the best birthday present ever."

"I'm so glad!" she said, turning the car key and making the engine roar. "We can go to all the Ocean World shows and eat whatever you want. It's a special day to celebrate you being such a great student this year."

As we drove, I looked around inside her car. It smelled like a mix of old upholstery and a hint of her perfume. The radio played rock and roll music. I wondered what it was like for her to drive this car every day. I daydreamed and imagined her singing along to rock and roll songs on the radio and thinking about her students.

"Do you like Ocean World, Miss Shelton?" I asked, curious to know what she would say.

"I love it!" she said. "I haven't been in a while. I used to go with my family when I was a kid. It's such fun. Today, it's all about having the best time."

She glanced at me with a smile.

"I'm really excited," I said. "I told my best friend Perry about it, but he couldn't come. I feel bad saying this, but I'm kinda glad he couldn't come because I get to spend the whole day with you," I said, feeling my cheeks heat up.

"That's sweet, Anthony," she said in a gentle voice. "I'm happy to spend the day with you too. I know it's been a tough few months for you, and I wanted to make sure you had something fun and special to look forward to."

She was driving with one hand on the wheel and one hand on the radio volume, turning the music lower. We chatted about everything—what I liked about school, our favorite animals, and what we were excited to see at Ocean World. Miss Shelton told me about her week. I listened closely, absorbing all of it.

I felt grateful to be in her car on the way to Ocean World. It felt unreal.

"Do you want to stop at 7-Eleven for a Slurpee on the way?" she suddenly asked.

"I would love to, but I've had so many Slurpees lately. My Uncle Bernie takes us after school sometimes, and we get Wacky Packages too," I said, smiling.

"My mom makes sure we don't have too much sugar before lunch," I said.

"She sounds very progressive," Miss Shelton said.

"She is," I said. "We eat turkey burgers and beef hot dogs. She knows all the healthy food trends. She says variety is important, so I can have Slurpees too."

"We can get one on the way back if you feel like it," she said.

"I would love that," I said with a big smile.

As we neared Ocean World, my excitement grew. The entrance loomed ahead, and I could see the iconic, big Ocean World sign in the distance. Miss Shelton parked the car and turned to me.

"Ready to have the best day ever?" she asked.

"Yes! Let's go!" I practically shouted, my heart racing with anticipation.

We spent the day watching shows, exploring exhibits, and laughing together. We started with the dolphin show, with Pepper, Diana, and Dimples jumping through hoops, flying from the pool, and doing tricks in the air, splashing the audience and performing incredible tricks. Miss Shelton and I laughed as we got drenched, and I was amazed at the show finale, when six dolphins skimmed along the water on their tails.

After that, we saw the sea lions, Thumper and Cleopatra, playing it up for the crowd with their trainers. Miss Shelton had bought us some popcorn and cotton candy. We sat near the front of the audience, enjoying the performance.

"What's your favorite part of Ocean World so far?" she asked while handing me a cone of cotton candy.

"It has to be the dolphins. They're so smart and fun to watch," I said, taking a big bite of the blue treat. "I love the sea lions too."

"I agree. The dolphins are amazing. They're so smart. I've always had a soft spot for them," she said, smiling.

I told her I had learned so much about dolphins in her class and it made me more curious about other sea animals.

"My favorite football team is the Miami Dolphins," I said during a break in the sea lion show. "I met two of my favorite players, Larry Csonka and Jim Kiick, who are both running backs, last month. They were signing autographs out in front of the 7-Eleven right by our school!"

She smiled at my enthusiasm and gave my shoulder a squeeze. I was in heaven.

We walked through the aquarium next, where we saw colorful fish, sharks, and even a giant sea turtle. I pressed my face against the glass, fascinated by the underwater world. Miss Shelton was beside me, pointing out different species and telling me interesting facts.

"You know a lot about sea animals," I said, impressed.

"I've always loved the ocean. When I was in college, I took a few marine biology courses. It's such a fascinating subject," she explained.

"I want to learn more about it too. Maybe I can study marine biology one day," I said, feeling inspired.

"You'd be great at it, Anthony. You're a very bright and curious student. I've really enjoyed having you in my class this year," she said, her eyes smiling.

"Thanks, Miss Shelton. I've loved being in your class too. You make learning so much fun," I said, feeling happy.

The day flew by as we explored exhibits and watched shows. We saw sea lions perform tricks, touched starfish in their pool, and rode some rides. Miss Shelton made sure we did everything we wanted to do, and I felt like the luckiest kid in the world for the day.

As we talked and walked to her car, I was buzzing from the fun.

On the drive back, I was tired and happy.

Miss Shelton turned to me with a thoughtful look on her face.

"Anthony, how's everything at home? Has it gotten any better since your dad, Nick, is out of the picture now?" she asked.

I hesitated, not sure how much to share. "It's a little better. Mom seems happier. It's still hard sometimes. Robert and Donna fight sometimes, and Mom is tired a lot."

Miss Shelton nodded. She seemed concerned. "How's your mom doing? It must be tough for her too."

"She's okay, I guess. She works a lot and complains about the house. She's strong. She always makes sure we're taken care of," I said, feeling a surge of protectiveness toward my mom.

"That's good to hear. It's important to have a strong family, even when things are tough," she said. "I remember when my parents divorced. It was hard on my mom too.

She had to work two jobs to make ends meet, but she never gave up."

"Your parents divorced?" I asked, surprised. I had never heard about her personal life before.

"Yes, when I was about your age. It was a difficult time, but it made us closer. My mom and I have a very special bond because of it," she said in a soft voice.

"I'm glad you have that," I said, feeling more connected to her. "Thank you, Anthony. And I'm glad you have your mom. She sounds wonderful," she said.

As we talked, I felt like Miss Shelton was a real person, not just as my teacher but as an actual person. This was the first time I could see a teacher like I would see another grown up.

It felt unreal. And I felt like she valued what I was saying.

"I've really enjoyed teaching you this year, Anthony. You're such a bright and hardworking student. You make me proud every day," she said sweetly.

"I enjoy it too, Miss Shelton. You're my favorite teacher. You make learning things so interesting," I said, feeling grateful.

I was sad when her car pulled into the driveway. Sad that the day with her was ending. I thought about telling her I would remember this day forever. Instead, I said thanks.

"Thank you, Miss Shelton. This was the best birthday ever," I said as I opened the car door.

"I'm so glad you had fun, Anthony. You deserve it," she said with a warm, wide smile.

As I waved goodbye and watched her car drive away, I said in my head, *I'll remember this day forever.*

I journaled about it, in the journal Mrs. Richter gave me in third grade.

"This day wasn't just about Ocean World or my birthday—it was about getting to know Miss Shelton," I wrote in my journal.

"Such an amazing gift for my birthday."

CHAPTER 17

Crossing Guard

5th Grade

"ANTHONY, COME OVER HERE."

Mr. Jenkins's voice carried across the empty street, drawing my attention from my post. He was my fifth-grade teacher. We students called him a gentle giant.

He was glaring at me, standing on the steps of his portable classroom. Our portable classroom. His tall frame cast a long shadow in the late afternoon sun.

"Mr. Jenkins, I can't. I have to stay at my station," I replied, glancing at the now-empty street where kids had crossed. I checked my watch. There were still 15 minutes left on my crossing guard shift. I looked back at Mr. Jenkins. He knew what I was thinking.

He chuckled deeply. "You don't have to stay over there, Anthony. Come over here. It's 45 minutes after school. There's no one else to cross the street."

"I know, but I might get in trouble," I said with a sigh.

"I'll make sure you don't get in trouble," he reassured me with a slight grin that didn't quite reach his eyes. I knew he knew the head of the crossing guard team at North Lauderdale Elementary—Mrs. Martinez—but I also knew he didn't think I was in any danger of getting in trouble.

Despite his towering six-foot-two frame, which made him look like a linebacker from my favorite football team, the Miami Dolphins, I hesitated to leave my post.

Standing with my orange strap across my chest and my black-and-silver "School Crossing Guard" badge over my heart, I turned to look at Mr. Jenkins.

Slowly, I began to walk toward the stairs of the portable building where Mr. Jenkins stood. The school had been recently built, and in second grade, we moved from the portables to these classrooms when the school building officially opened three years ago. North Lauderdale kept growing, so they had to add portables in the area around the school, as we outgrew the school building, which was only a couple of years old.

The bright South Florida sun heated up the plastic badge through the orange material it was pinned to, so I was happy to move toward the shade of the portable classroom steps where Mr. Jenkins stood.

I took pride in my North Lauderdale Elementary School badge, which looked just like a police badge. I lifted the orange vest over my head and smiled at it as I walked over.

Mr. Jenkins's portable classroom, like the others, was a rectangular structure with beige siding and small windows. The portable was mostly unattractive. The exterior was plain, with stairs leading up to the entrance. The portable sat on concrete blocks, slightly elevated from the ground, surrounded by a patch of grass here and there, many rocks, and so much dirt.

As I stepped inside, the cool blast of air conditioning was a welcome relief from the hot South Florida sun. The inside of the portable was a mix of practicality and personality. The walls were filled with educational posters, such as multiplication tables, a map of the United States, and a large cursive alphabet strip running along the top of the chalkboard.

Mr. Jenkins's desk showed his organized and approachable nature. Neatly stacked papers and lesson plans were offset by a few personal items, such as a framed photo of his family and a Miami Dolphins mug. There were small plants to add green, my favorite color, all around our classroom. There were also a few comic books and magazines—*Rolling Stone* and *National Geographic*—showing his interests. He had a *Star Wars* movie poster and a Superman poster hanging up.

The classroom was empty, as the school day was over. It was just the two of us.

"Why do you talk so much in class?" Mr. Jenkins asked.

He surprised me with his direct question.

I didn't hesitate to answer. At the beginning of the school year, I was afraid of him. Now that it was a couple of months into the school year, almost Halloween, he felt familiar, almost like a dad.

"Sorry, Mr. Jenkins, but I have to talk because if I don't talk, Jenny's gonna be with Frank. She sits right next to him," I explained. "Because he's next to her, he talks to her a lot more than I do. If he talks to her more, he's gonna win."

Mr. Jenkins laughed. He didn't laugh often in class, but I was glad he was laughing a lot today. It made me feel like I could tell him almost anything.

"I get it, Anthony. I get it," he said with a side smile. "But you're making my job harder."

I noticed he wasn't smiling but looking me right in the eyes. His honest look made me feel good, even though I felt like I wasn't going to like what he was going to say.

"My job is to make sure that you don't talk in class," he said with a stare.

He saw I heard him clearly. His whole face then broke into a wide smile.

"So, Frank is going to win because he sits right next to her?"

"Yes," I said.

"Where do you sit?"

"Behind her."

"What's the difference?"

I looked at him and shrugged.

"I don't want to get in the way of your competition," he chuckled again, "but if you keep talking to her from behind her, I'm going to have to move you further back."

I was surprised he said this. I thought he was rooting for me to win over Jenny. I realized he was not.

"I like you to be closer to the front of the class because you raise your hand a lot, but if you don't stop talking to Jenny so much, I'm gonna move you."

He's our teacher first, I thought. *I get it.*

"I understand, Mr. Jenkins, but if you switch my seat with Frank and I sit next to Jenny, then I could whisper or talk less. I would be right next to her!"

Now he was smiling wider. "Anthony, I appreciate your eagerness in asking for what you want. You are a charming, confident young man. I like that about you. But I'm not going to move Frank. He needs to be up front to understand what I'm saying in class.

I'm simply telling you to stop talking in class or I'm going to move you. Case closed."

"Got it, Mr. Jenkins."

I didn't like what he was saying, but I liked that he was so honest with me.

He looked at me for an extra second or two. He took a step back and put his hands in his pockets.

"So, how are things going at home?"

"They are getting a little better. My dad is gone."

"Where is he?"

"We don't know. There was a court hearing and he didn't show up. I went there to be with my mom and answer questions that the judge asked."

"That's really good that you are there for your mom," Mr.

Jenkins said. "Always be there for your mom. She's your number one lady. Remember that!"

"I will, Mr. Jenkins. I'm happy to help. I'm so nervous though."

He took a moment and thought to himself before asking me questions.

"Did the judge ask you a lot of questions?"

"He did. So many. I don't remember all the questions. I just remember being really worried as I was answering."

"Did your mom help? Was she able to speak?"

"Not really. She did help me, though," I said. "She told me in the car on the way to the courthouse what to say to the judge. I told her I was worried I was going to say something wrong, and she told me not to worry."

Mr. Jenkins nodded, his eyes filled with understanding. "It sounds like you're doing a great job handling things at home, Anthony. Just keep being there for your mom. She needs you."

As he spoke, I felt so many emotions. I was grateful for his concern and advice, but it was hard to think about Nick and everything that had happened.

Mr. Jenkins's words reminded me that even though things were tough, I had to stay strong for my mom.

"I will, Mr. Jenkins. Thanks for talking with me."

He patted me on the shoulder, his hand warm and reassuring.

"Anytime, Anthony. Now, go finish your shift. I don't want to get you in trouble with Mrs. Martinez."

I nodded and smiled, feeling a bit lighter as I headed back to my post. Even though my situation at home was difficult, knowing I had someone like Mr. Jenkins looking out for me made it a little easier.

The next morning, I walked into Mr. Jenkins's portable classroom, feeling the cool air conditioning wash over me as I stepped inside. The air was filled with the faint scent of chalk and fresh paper. The walls, decorated with educational posters and pop culture references, made the room feel full of life and welcoming. There was a new addition today, a vibrant poster of *Grease*, the hit movie that had just come out that year.

Mr. Jenkins stood at the front of the classroom, writing the day's agenda on the chalkboard. His neat handwriting spelled out our schedule, and he even included a not-so-great doodle of John Travolta and Olivia Newton-John from the movie *Grease*.

The room buzzed with the chatter of my classmates as they settled into their seats. We all start laughing at the doodle, not sure if it was supposed to be funny or not but giggling anyway. Mr. Jenkins didn't seem like a doodler.

As he turned back to the chalkboard, I glanced over at Jenny just in front of me.

Frank, who usually occupied the seat next to her, was absent—maybe in the bathroom?

Seizing the opportunity, I leaned forward.

"Hey, Jenny," I whispered. "Did you get the math homework done?"

Jenny turned slightly with a big smile. "Yeah, I did. It was tricky, though. Did you finish yours?"

"Mostly," I replied, trying to sound confident. "But I got stuck on the last problem. Maybe we can go over it together later?"

"Sure," she said, her smile widening. "I'd like that."

Just then, I saw Mr. Jenkins looking directly at me, his expression a mix of sternness and humor. He gave a small nod—a clear reminder of our conversation yesterday. I straightened up immediately and focused on my notebook, feeling a little embarrassed but also grateful for the silent warning.

"All right, let's review some of the key points from yesterday's lesson," Mr. Jenkins said. His tone was firm, commanding our attention. "Anthony, can you tell us the answer to problem three on page forty-two?"

I quickly flipped through my textbook, finding the problem. "Um, it's 36," I said, hoping I'd got it right.

"Correct," Mr. Jenkins said with a nod. "Good job. Now, Jenny, can you explain how we get that answer?"

Jenny gave a quick and clear answer. As she spoke, I couldn't help but feel a mix of admiration and a funny feeling in my stomach.

I stayed quiet, remembering Mr. Jenkins's words from the day before.

As the lesson continued, I kept my focus on the board and my notebook. Occasionally, I glanced at Jenny, and we exchanged quick smiles. I knew I had to stay quiet during class, but our silent communication felt meaningful too.

When the bell rang, signaling the end of the period, Mr. Jenkins gave me a nod and a small smile. I smiled back, feeling a sense of accomplishment. Even though I didn't get to talk to Jenny much, I knew I did the right thing.

As I walked out of the classroom, I felt more confident, knowing that Mr. Jenkins was looking out for me, both in the classroom and out.

CHAPTER 18

A Party to Remember

5th Grade Summer

"CAPTAIN CAAAVEMAAAANNNN!" I HEARD FROM THE LIVING ROOM. Robert and Donna were already up, watching Saturday morning cartoons. I heard them talking as the show played. I was excited to wake up to Captain Caveman shouting his rally cry.

The South Florida sun was already shining brightly through the bedroom window. I was feeling excited and a little nervous as I got out of bed. I looked over at my Hulk figurine, sitting on my dresser just under my mirror, and smiled.

He's been there for a few months now, I thought as I looked at his face, all scrunched up and dark green. His messy dark black hair hung slightly on his forehead. For the first time, I noticed he wasn't smiling. *He always looks agitated*, I thought. I smiled, wishing they made one where his face would change and maybe smile every now and then.

I opened my drawer and looked for clothes to wear.

Today was Jenny's birthday party! I had been looking forward to it ever since she handed me the invitation, all pink and sparkly with a drawing she made of a birthday cake on the front. I smiled when I got it, thinking about how much fun we'd have at her party. And now it was the day! Jenny and I had become good friends that year. Lately, I'd noticed I liked being around her even more than before.

I arrived at Jenny's house, excited. Her house was nicer than any place I'd ever been. It was built in one of those developments near our school, with freshly paved streets and colorful flowers in the yard. She had sunflowers along the path to her front door. I hadn't seen those much. The whole house was white with a light brown trim that made it look, well, happy. I had never thought a house looked happy before.

Her house had a red front door. The two cars in the driveway looked like they had just come from the dealership. Never had I seen a place so perfect.

Inside, the party was in full swing. Kids from our class were running around, laughing, and playing games. The kitchen was filled with food and the smell of pizza, and a big bowl of fruit sat on the counter, waiting for dessert time. Jenny's mom had set out a tray of vegetables—carrots, celery, and cucumbers—but I noticed most of the kids, including me, were more interested in pizza and fruit. We heard there would be ice cream cake later.

I spotted Jenny across the room, her bright eyes eager as she talked with a group of girls from school. She looked over and waved, then came over to me.

"Hey, Anthony! I'm so glad you came!" she said, her voice cheerful and kind.

"Wouldn't miss it," I replied, trying to sound cool but feeling my face heat up a bit. Jenny had that effect on me, making me both nervous and happy at the same time.

As the party went on, I noticed Frank hovering around Jenny. Frank sat next to her in class, and I knew he had the same idea I did—to spend as much time with Jenny as possible. Whenever he tried to join our conversations, Jenny would politely answer him and then turn back to me. It made me feel special, like I had her attention more than anyone else.

At one point, Jenny introduced me to her dad.

"Hey, Dad, this is Anthony, the guy from school I've been telling you about," she said with a grin.

Her dad, a tall man with a stern look, shook my hand. "Nice to meet you, Anthony," he said, his voice deep and a bit gruff. I could tell he was sizing me up, and I felt a bit nervous under his gaze.

"It's nice to meet you too, sir," I replied, doing my best to sound respectful.

He asked me about my family, and I found myself talking about how things had changed for the better recently.

"My mom's doing a lot better now," I began. "She met a guy, Carl, who's really great! They met at work, in a dental lab. He's so good to us. It's been a lot nicer at home."

Jenny's dad nodded, listening, though he looked a bit uncomfortable. I thought, *Maybe I'm sharing too much*, so I asked him, "What do you do for work, sir?"

He looked relieved at the shift. "I work in finance," he said simply. I think he believed that explained everything. I didn't really know what that meant, but it sounded important.

Jenny's mom was quiet. I noticed her watching Jenny and me from the kitchen. She brought over a plate with a slice of pizza. She smiled at me, and I noticed she had the same gentle eyes as Jenny. I couldn't remember her mom's name, but she seemed nice. She didn't say much, so I figured it was better not to say too much either, especially after sharing so much with her dad.

As we all gathered around the table for cake, I made sure to sing the loudest during the "Happy Birthday" song. Jenny grinned at me when I hit the high note, and I felt warmth in my chest. The cake was a Carvel ice cream cake, my favorite. It felt like Jenny and I had this special connection, even down to our favorite desserts.

After the cake, Jenny's dad played a prank on me. He pointed to a small pepper plant on the windowsill. "Hey, Anthony, have you ever tried one of these peppers?" he asked with a playful twinkle in his eye.

I looked at the tiny peppers, not wanting to back down in front of Jenny or her dad. "No, but how bad could they be?" I said. I picked one, shrugged, and popped it into my mouth. The burn hit almost immediately, and I felt my eyes water. I tried to play it cool, but I could see Jenny's dad watching me closely.

"Pretty spicy, huh?" he said with a chuckle.

"Yeah," I somehow got the word out, then quickly gulping down a glass of water Jenny handed me. She had run over to grab a glass of water for me almost immediately, I noticed.

Everyone laughed, and even though my mouth felt like it was on fire, I couldn't help but join in and laugh too. It was fun to be part of the joke, even if I was the punch line.

As the party started winding down, Jenny pulled me aside. "Can you stay a little longer?" she asked, her eyes hopeful.

I nodded. "I asked my mom to pick me up later, just in case," I said with a grin, glad I had thought ahead. I wanted to spend as much time with Jenny as possible.

We sat on the front porch, talking about everything and nothing. Jenny told me her parents had been married for years and how lucky she felt to have a stable family. I nodded, feeling a bit envious but happy for her.

"You're lucky," I said. "My life's been kinda crazy. It's getting better. Since Nick left, things have been . . . peaceful."

Jenny looked at me sympathetically. "I'm glad you're doing better," she said softly. "You've been through a lot."

I swallowed hard, feeling a lump in my throat. It was nice to have someone who cared. She was one of the first friends I felt I could share my whole life with. It felt good to be able to share with her, almost like a weight had been lifted off.

I noticed I was much more comfortable sharing my story and the story of my family now that it felt like the worst was over. When things were bad early in grade school, I felt like I shouldn't tell anyone about it because maybe someone would try to help, and I was worried that authorities would break up our family somehow. Also, I didn't want to burden anyone with all of my troubles. Plus, I was somewhat ashamed of all that was going on. I felt like I should hide it.

Now, I was surprised by how okay I was with sharing openly.

"Yeah, but I'm okay. My mom's happy now, and Carl's been great. He's like the dad we never had," I said. Then I joked, "Well, we did have one, but then we didn't, and now maybe we do... "

She smiled and took my hand, squeezing it gently. "You're strong, Anthony. Not everyone could go through what you did and still be so... nice."

I felt my face heat up again, but this time it was from her words. "Thanks," I mumbled, looking down. "It helps to have good friends. And good teachers, like Mr. Jenkins."

Jenny nodded. "Yeah, Mr. Jenkins is the best. He's so quiet and serious, but you can tell he really cares. He makes school feel like a fun, safe place."

I agreed. Mr. Jenkins had been a steady presence in my life, a calm force in a stormy year. "He's a good guy," I said. "I'm glad we have him for fifth grade. He's there just when we need him."

Before I knew it, my mom's car pulled up to the curb. Jenny walked me to the car, holding my hand. As we reached the car, she smiled at my mom. "Hi! We had so much fun today! Anthony's great."

My mom smiled back, her eyes warm. "I'm glad to hear that, Jenny. It's nice to see him happy." I saw them exchange quiet smiles. I felt a wave of gratitude through my body.

"That's my mom, Jackie," I said awkwardly to Jenny, not sure how to say goodbye.

"Hi, Jackie," Jenny said to my mom with a sweet, warm smile as she reached over and squeezed my hand.

I squeezed back.

When I got in the car, I waved goodbye to Jenny, feeling a little sad to leave but happy with how the day had gone. As we drove away, I looked at my mom, excited to tell her all about the party. She glanced at me and smiled, as if she already knew how much it meant to me to be there.

"Her family is so nice, Mom," I said. "Her dad is in finance, and her mom is kind to me, just like Jenny. And they had Carvel cake, just like the one I like for my birthday," I said excitedly.

"I'm so glad they invited you over," my mom said. "They sound like they have a perfect family."

"Ours is perfect too, Mom," I said with a smile, and I meant it.

"Well, it has been bumpy," she said with a laugh and a sigh. "Bumpy with a side of bumps."

We both laughed. We laughed hard.

"I'll take all of the bumps, Mom," I said. "I like the road we're on."

She glanced at me, smiling, then looked back at the road.

"So much of it is stuff that nobody sees," she said. "The struggle is real."

"I'm just glad that you, Robert, Donna, and I are still together," I said. "I always worry about that."

"I don't worry so much anymore," she said. "I juggle a lot and so much happens that I don't expect, but I'm not going to let anything like that happen again."

I relaxed in the front seat of the car, held tight by my seatbelt. I closed my eyes for a moment, reflecting on the day.

As we drove home, I went over the birthday party in my head. It was a glimpse into a world where things seemed easy and simple. A world where I could relax and be a kid, with a friend who liked me for who I was and a family that seemed in harmony.

I looked at my mom, appreciating all that she did to get through all that she and we had to get through. *She's so tough,* I thought. Our life wasn't easy and simple, but it was the life I knew and the life I loved.

As we pulled into our driveway, I felt a sense of peace.

Taking Jenny's cue, I reached over to my mom's hand when she pulled the keys from the ignition.

"I love you, Mom," I said. "And I appreciate all you do. Even the things we don't see."

She smiled at me.

And just like that, the day was over.

Things were getting better, one day at a time. And I knew, deep down, no matter what, I would be okay. We would be okay.

I had my family, my friends, and a future that looked brighter than before.

And for now, that was enough.

Acknowledgments

I WOULD LIKE TO THANK ALL OF THE TEACHERS NAMED IN THIS book for giving me love, attention, and care during my grade school years. Huge kudos and a heartfelt thank you to all of my teachers for seeing there was a need, and so wonderfully and gracefully filling it.

To my grade school teachers: You are champions. I am and always will remain grateful. If they or anyone in their families reads this book, please reach out to me at *anthony@hianthony.com*. I would love to hear from you.

A big thank you to my older brother, Robert, and younger sister, Donna, for being warriors during our grade school years and throughout our lives. It readied us for challenges ahead. We stood together during those early years and you both, then and now, provide a rock-solid foundation. I love you both so much.

An exquisite thank you to my amazing kids, Logan and Gabby. You show me what true love is every day. Your resilience and strength impresses me. It's one of life's greatest gifts and such a delight to watch you both grow from babies to teenagers. Keep showing me how it's done. I learn from you both each day.

Watching my kids grow with so much love from our family, friends, and, of course, their wonderful teachers, helped inspire me to write this book. Thank you to these teachers, faculty and staff for your uniquely helpful and thoughtful support, which put a spotlight on how important teachers are for all of us.

Finally, to my hometown North Lauderdale Elementary in South Florida and the teachers and administrators there now— keep up the good work.

To all teachers: Thank you for supporting, teaching, and inspiring us all.

We, your students, feel you throughout our lives.

The world needs more teachers.

About the Author

ANTHONY MASSUCCI is an author and former Bloomberg News and Time Warner AOL Daily Finance journalist and Bloomberg TV broadcaster. For the past decade he has run his own media firm, HiAnthony Media.
He lives in Manhattan, New York, with his son and daughter.

To learn more about the author, please visit *HiAnthony.com*.

www.ingramcontent.com/pod-product-compliance
Lightning Source LLC
Chambersburg PA
CBHW020417150626
46554CB00014B/1908